MAN-MADE
The Chronicles of Our Extraterrestrial Gods

Rita Louise and Wayne Laiberte have mined the valuable resource of the world's traditional systems of wisdom to help us understand our origins and destiny. They conclude we are not the product of chance combinations of matter acted upon by natural selection. Rather we are the product of what they call "unnatural selection," by which they mean the intelligent action of higher beings. This understanding has major implications for our human civilization.
Michael A. Cremo, author of Forbidden Archeology

"Man-Made" is an exquisite interweaving of cross-cultural creation legends going back millions of years that uncovers a startling new perspective: These global stories may actually be records of the intervention of the sky gods in human evolution! We think of the creation stories as cherished reports by early humans, so this reverse perspective generates startling new ideas. For example, the authors wonder if the nearly total cleansing of our species during the Flood is actually a record kept by the gods of Neanderthal extinction! A thoroughly engrossing epic sweep through millions of years of evolution grounded in sound science and excellent storytelling, "Man-Made" is a must-read for all students of myth and global creation stories.
Barbara Hand Clow, author of Awakening the Planetary Mind

A work of impressive research and thought-provoking analysis, Man Made: The Chronicles of Our Extraterrestrial Gods by Rita Louise and Wayne Laliberte traces the story of human evolution as told in the myths and legends of all cultures. These multicultural creation myths prove to be as truth-telling as the "facts" disclosed by our sciences of archaeology, anthropology, and geology. Most astonishing, the authors state that their findings reveal that the stories the ancient myths proclaim are not only the accounts of human history, but the revelations and the chronicles of the gods themselves.
Brad Steiger, author of Worlds Before Our Own; Atlantis Rising.

Based on a comparative study of myths from around the world, and weaving in data from genetics, archaeology, anthropology, cosmology, and many other disciplines, Rita Louise and Wayne Laliberté come to the firm conclusion: "The gods who came to this Earth and created life on this planet were living breathing beings." Absolutely fascinating and a must read for anyone interested in the "extraterrestrial question" of the origins of humanity.
Robert M. Schoch, Ph.D., author of Forgotten Civilization

"With "Man-Made," Dr. Rita Louise and Wayne Laliberte have made an incalculable contribution to our understanding of humanity's true past, and with it, provided a glimpse into what may be a fast approaching, exciting new future of truth."
Mike Bara, author of *Ancient Aliens On The Moon*

In Man Made: The Chronicles Of Our Extraterrestrial Gods, Dr. Rita Louise and Wayne Laliberte take us on a fantastic and mystery-filled journey into the ancient past and the dawning of human civilization. It's a journey that encompasses, gods, aliens (or are they one and the same?), ancient mythology, amazing legend, and even more amazing revelations concerning our origins as a species. As Dr. Rita and Wayne demonstrate, the world and history we think we know doesn't even come close...
Nick Redfern, author of *The Pyramids and the Pentagon*

An epic book evidencing extensive research probing into our past presenting a congruent theory spanning ancient creation myths from all over the world. Retells a plethora of interwoven stories exposing power-hungry gods from ancient times battling for control of the Earth from Babylon, China, India, Egypt, Mexico, and Africa. Offers new perspectives of biblical verses and deciphers legends of 'the shining ones', avatars, dwarfs, giants, 'Sky People', winged war-horses and fallen angels. Exposes dissension and conflict amongst the gods and massive evolutionary leaps in the fossil record showing synchronicities and parallels in time. Come and be intrigued with tales of magic potions, distended skulls, and eternal youth.
Dr Carmen Boulter, director and producer of *The Pyramid Code* TV series

Man-Made is a truly enjoyable, informative, and well-researched overview of the concept of ancient gods and their mythical relationships to humanity, as seen through the eyes of widespread cultures.
Laird Scranton, author of *The Science of the Dogon*

From their analysis of the Progenitors, to their look at the Golden Age, this book by Dr. Rita Louise and Wayne Laliberte is arguably one of the most solid attempts to uncover dark and hidden truths about us
Anthony F. Sanchez, author of *UFO Highway*

"Man-Made" is a flight throughout our mythology and legends, inviting the reader to look at it with new, wide-open eyes.
Philip Coppens - Author of *The Ancient Alien Question*

MAN-MADE©

The Chronicles of Our
Extraterrestrial Gods

Rita Louise, PhD &
Wayne Laliberté, MS

ISBN # 978-0-9758649-1-3

Library of Congress Control Number: 2012911464

First Edition

Printed in the United States of America

Cover design:
Scott Alan Roberts
www.scottalanroberts.com

Cover image of Dr. Rita Louise
David McClary
www.ifgaphoto.com

This book is dedicated to my grandmother who came through in an on-air reading with psychic medium James Van Praggue as part of an interview on Just Energy Radio.

My grandmother in her typical style, and in no uncertain terms, told me to *"finish the book"!*

Thanks Gram - EVOL

Acknowledgements

We would like to thank our many friends whose encouragement, and keen interest in the topic, kept us moving forward. A special thanks to Philip Weidler whose suggestions early in the writing helped to simplify an already complex narrative.

Contents

Foreward

The one great question for humanity has always been: where do we come from? Great minds have wrestled with this since the dawn of consciousness, and various theories have been produced; some enduring and others not. Science has certain ideas, and religions others. But none are conclusive nor universally accepted.

The rise of Darwinism in the 19th century reputes to be the truth, from a left-brain perspective at least, that we are the product of a long line of evolution beginning with the simplest of life forms. Yet others insist we are the result of a conscious effort from some form of intelligence, be it a universal force we call God, or by gods from another part of the universe, or even a parallel one.

Many oral traditions of the indigenous people of the planet have stories involving the direct seeding of life, and in fact humanity from extraterrestrial visitors. In the case of authors such as Zecharia Sitchin, extraterrestrial visitors produced a slave race to do their labour, while others speak of ancestors coming from such star systems as the Pleiades and nurturing our biological and spiritual evolution in a loving way.

The honest truth is that no one really has a definitive answer. The Bible speaks of fallen angels and even giants seeding the daughters of men, and other ancient texts carry similar sayings.

For the greater part of the history of humanity, the keepers of such thoughts and knowledge have tended to be a small sector of the population in positions of power, mainly political and religious, and in more recent times, scientific. But thanks to the free flow of information, first through books, and now the internet, alternative

1

views from all over the planet are available to challenge the "powers that be" from being the controllers of our right to know and think freely as sovereign people.

The so-called "alternative" historians and researchers such as Graham Hancock with his ground-breaking book *Fingerprints Of The Gods,* questioned the orthodox understanding of our historical time line of who we are and where we come from. This book in particular definitely upset many orthodox researchers who almost vehemently oppose the idea that civilization, as we commonly know it, began more than 6000 years ago.

However, the enigmas remain, and challenge such narrow-minded thought patterns. Do they honestly still think that the great pyramid of Giza in Egypt was made by descendants of hunter-gatherers? And were the machined hard stone surfaces at Puma Punku near Lake Titicaca really the product of loin cloth wearing native people using stone hammers as depicted in the Tiwanaku museum in Bolivia?

Such strict adherence to worn out and somewhat childish ideas are now being challenged with science. Engineers such as Christopher Dunn, author of the Giza Power Plant has convincingly shown that the great pyramid in Egypt may have been a functioning power station built before the Pharaohs ever existed. And Dr. Robert Schoch of Boston University, geologist, has dated the Sphinx at being 7000 years old, at a minimum.

The old paradigms of who we are and where we come from are gradually, and increasingly, being challenged by hard evidence, and this is no longer the domain of a few elite individuals, or academics with clandestine peer groups.

And what of evolution? It has not been conclusively proven that humans are descended from ape like beings. In fact, thanks to the work of Lloyd Pye, best known for the Star Child Project, has pointed out that humans have 23 pairs of chromosomes, whereas the great apes have 24. How could this have occurred? Did some ancient people or visitors from off this planet have the capacity to manipulate our DNA?

2

This book by Dr. Rita Louise and Wayne Laliberte is timely and potent. Using science and oral traditions from around the world they present convincing evidence that who were are was not the result of simple evolution, but I will let you peruse this work and come to your own conclusions.

Brien Foerster
www.hiddenincatours.com

August 25 2012

Somewhere in Peru...

Introduction

It was the summer of 2009 that we, Wayne and I, watched a show on television exploring the Mayan Calendar and the purported events that were to transpire on December 21, 2012. Wayne and I are both alternative thought enthusiasts. We both enjoy exploring topics such as ancient mysteries, UFO's, and the paranormal. Many times while viewing television specials in these respective fields we find ourselves laughing aloud at contradictory claims made by many "experts" in their respective fields.

The narrator, at one point in the show we were watching identified cultures from around the world that supported the concepts associated with the Mayan Calendar and implied the end of a World Cycle in 2012. We noticed numerous references made to these "other cultures", yet no specific details were provided.

At first, we thought we had missed something. Perhaps we were discussing the potential parallels of the show to our mythic history research. Then again, we might have been lost in our own thoughts about the topic of discussion. In any case, we missed the supporting facts and found ourselves left with an unsatisfied curiosity.

Fortunately for us, the show repeated a few weeks later. We watched it again, I had pen and paper in hand waiting for the specific references to the other cultures, beliefs, and philosophies that we had obviously missed. Our second viewing of the show provided no additional insights. References to the Egyptian, Hindi, and Hopi traditions were made, but the subject was quickly changed and a new topic introduced. We joked with each other that we must have cat-like tendencies because our curiosity was immediately aroused. Thus, the digging began.

Our first stop was the Hindu classic, the Vishnu Purana. The Vishnu Purana goes into explicit detail regarding the creation of the world, the yuga cycles of time and the Hindu concept regarding the end of the current cycle we are in, the Kali Yuga. What we discovered was instead of the Kali Yuga ending in 2012, as implied in the show about the Mayan Calendar, it does not end for another 427,000 years. We found similar discrepancies when we investigated the works and writings of the Hopi Indians. We found ourselves disappointed in the knowledge that even television shows purporting alternative theories only provided the viewer with their brand of truth.

One offshoot in researching the reality of what was being presented was our introduction to a story in the Vishnu Purana of Manu and the fish. (We will be going into detail regarding Manu's story later in the text.) Briefly, the story tells how Matsya, the fish, saved Manu and humanity from a flood that devastated the Earth. Wayne and I were both familiar with the notion that cultures worldwide recount a flood myth, but we found ourselves taken aback with the story of Manu. The parallels, when placed next to the biblical story of Noah, were uncanny.

Our quest to ferret out real human history, through the eyes of mythology had begun.

Little did we know where this quest would take us. In order to make this journey, we were forced to put our preconceived notions to the side. We had to forget all we were taught in school and look at our distant past with fresh, unprejudiced eyes.

Our voyage took many unexpected twists and turns. Assumptions and revelations we made early on, were replaced by new ones. The more we learned, we found ourselves going deeper and deeper down the rabbit hole into a new paradigm of who we are and where we began. This process continued until we finally reached the last page of the book. It was only then that we could take a step back and see the whole story of our origin from start to finish.

Man-Made endeavors to solve a few parts of the puzzle of our history. It chronicles the myths of our ancestors and puts them into a cogent timeline of our past. We looked for parallels and common denominators in mythic traditions. Information we uncovered from one source was not included in the narrative unless we were able to find references to the same bit of information in another source to verify the veracity of the original claim. We did make one assumption. We presupposed that if multiple cultures were making the same claims, then there must be a hint of truth to what they were saying. Our discoveries were compared to current historical, archeological and scientific facts, many of which surprisingly supported the history we were unfolding. We made one other decision early in the writing of the text and that was to keep ourselves and our beliefs out of the narrative and instead "report the facts" as untainted and unbiased as possible. If we do provide conjecture, we try to identify them.

With our research concluded and the pieces of the puzzle put into place we were left with one unalterable conclusion: the folklore, legends and traditions we are about to share with you are not humanities stories about the gods, but instead the god's stories about THEIR lives, THEIR exploits and THEMSELVES. And what a story they tell...

Myth As History

When asked
"how do you know about the
generations of mankind and the
creation of men and women?"

The Aztecs replied:
"Quetzalcoatl told them".

The Babylonians said:
"it was the Oannes".

The Box

What holds a cultural group together? Is this glue a combination of their customs and beliefs? Could it be the foods they eat, the way they dress or perhaps the habits they have? Each of these mesh together to identify us and our place in the world. Social groups and cultural norms establish the customs in our lives.

Pressure to conform to the norm (or rules) is true in any kind of personal organization, whether professional, educational or spiritual. In order to fit in, we submit ourselves to the extreme power of "group norms". We are often bullied, managed or controlled by the group. They can manipulate our thoughts, beliefs and view of the world. The key to social success in any group is conformity in what we think, say and do.

We do not normally recognize the impact social pressures have on us or how group norms can manipulate our choices and decisions. It was not long ago that sporting a tattoo was viewed as socially incorrect. Individuals with tattoos were avoided because they represented the shadier side of society. Many assumed that the tattooed individual was bad, evil or somehow dangerous. Today, tattooing has become a fad-like social norm for both men and women.

In a 2008 article in the Los Angeles Times, Shari Roan reported that about 93% of women who had indulged in getting a tattoo felt stigmatized as a result of their tattoos. About 40% of these women felt as if they had to endure negative comments at work or in public versus 20% and 5% of men respectively. This has led many women to decide to have their tattoos removed. The article suggests (ah...yes, even more control by the experts and the media) that women should think long and hard about where they get their tattoos placed. It goes on to suggest that perhaps they should select an area they could cover.

In the Western world we have been brainwashed into one way of thinking about ourselves. When we hear of something that is "outside the box" (i.e. the boundaries created by our social organizations), we often assess this breach of our norms with skepticism, disbelief, dislike or hate. Since the concept did not come from "one of us" we automatically assume it must be flawed. This is true especially if it contradicts our current beliefs or the beliefs of our social group.

Much of what we think and believe has been spoon-fed to us from the first day following birth. Case in point...Who discovered America? I will bet you are saying to yourself that question is easy, Christopher Columbus. Are you sure? Think about it again and use the contradictory historical facts you know are true. The Native Americans were here long before Columbus! Then there were the Vikings! According to Nordic tradition Bjarni Herjolfsson, a Norse settler in Greenland, sighted a continent west of Greenland when he was blown off course. Leif Eriksson and many others after him, not much after Bjarni's discovery, explored this new continent they called "Vinland". All of this transpired at least 500 years before Columbus spotted land on that fateful day. It might be interesting to ask someone from Scandinavia who discovered America. Would their response also be Christopher Columbus? Are their norms flawed?

The same holds true in non-Western countries. In nations such as India and China the thoughts, beliefs and traditions they share are vastly different from ours. The same can be said about ancient cultures. They believed in a world far different from what we were taught and hold to be true.

How did we get ourselves into such a mess? How did we become so separated from our origin, our past? The schism started in 325 CE when the Council of Nicaea put its stamp of approval upon the canonized books of the Christian Bible. This started Western society's break from fact. A chasm formed between what was fact in the ancient world and what was deemed appropriate and true by the Nicene Council. And then, the destruction of the Library of Alexandria ultimately sealed our fate.

The Library of Alexandra was established in Egypt around 300 BCE. It was designed to be a storehouse of ancient knowledge. Through a well-funded and aggressive directive, Egyptians, while under Greek rule, were charged with collecting knowledge from around the world. The vast amounts of ancient wisdom that was lost when the library burned is anyone's guess. There are several theories as to how or why the library ended up in ruin. These theories include a fire during the Alexandrian War in 48 BCE, a decree of the Coptic Pope Theophilus in 391 CE and the Muslim conquest in 642 CE. If you are interested in conspiracy theories, this ancient mystery is one that is yet unsolved.

The net result was that many of the documents that recorded our distant past were lost. What was left was a few pages of biblical text. Anything that fell outside its black and white lines was considered heretical. It did not take long before social stigma as well as persecutions in the name of "God" caused us to close our eyes to anything that went against the approved ways. Sadly, the Catholic Church is not the only one to use religious doctrine as a form of social control. The Romans persecuted the Catholics. The Catholics persecuted everyone... and the Jews, over the millennia, seemed always to be the subject of persecution.

Our connection to our ancient past took another blow during the Dark Ages, which began with the fall of the Roman Empire in the 5th century CE. The Catholic Church gained strength and increasingly dominated the lives of the people who lived during this time. The church became rich and powerful, which enabled them to influence and at times completely control the rulers of Europe.

From birth to death, the people of the Dark Ages lived in fear of excommunication. Excommunication from the church meant that when you died you would spend eternity suffering in the fires of hell. This religious programming forced people to live inside the box prescribed for them. Out of fear, they hid their true feelings and were reluctant to vocalize any thoughts that might have differed from church edicts.

People who strayed from the tried and true were condemned as heretics. Punishment for heresy included imprisonment, torture or execution. The rise of Catharism, a Gnostic form of Christianity, in the 12th century caused the persecution of heretics to become more frequent. Pope Gregory IX, in the 13th century, began assigning individuals from the Dominican Order the duty of judging individuals suspected of heresy. So began the Inquisitions. By the end of the century, a Grand Inquisitor was assigned to each proceeding. The most famous inquisitor was the Spanish Dominican, Tomás de Torquemada, who headed the Spanish Inquisition, whose name has become synonymous with the horrors of the Christian Inquisition.

The church controlled every aspect of people's lives for over 1,000 years. This control included their religious beliefs but also bled over into the sciences. The Pope, during this time, was solely responsible for interpreting the Bible. He did not have modern technology such as radio carbon dating, to identify the period in which an item was originally used. He did not have DNA testing to evaluate the differences between one species and another, nor did he have the Hubble Space Telescope to look out into the vastness of space and identify our place in it. He also did not possess the knowledge of gravity, electricity or the make-up of the subatomic world we take for granted today. His interpretations were based upon the facts of the day and assumptions he made.

The dawning of the Renaissance changed all of that. Starting in the middle of the 14th century, the Renaissance brought about a resurgence in the study of the science and philosophy of the ancient Greeks and Romans. This opened the door to entirely new thoughts. Well, not new thoughts, but ones that had not been explored or expressed in the Western world for centuries.

Even with the new and wonderful insights gained during the Renaissance, the damage was already done. The Bible, as both history and science, had established the very foundation for society in the Western world. This foundation was built upon assumptions made by someone, somewhere, and are based upon what these individuals learned, heard or read. It was not built upon science or even pseudoscience. Much of it was based upon superstition and conjecture.

Today, discoveries in the areas of astronomy, archeology, genetics and many other of the sciences directly conflict with the Bible. This divergence leaves many of us increasingly confused. We, the authors, do not question what the Bible says. What we question is its interpretation. Through our investigation into the past, we have found that the facts presented in the Bible can work very well with current science if the prevailing interpretation is removed or at the least, reassessed.

Here is an example of how an interpretation of the Bible formed the basis of scientific thought for hundreds of years. In 1650 CE, a Bishop named James Ussher tried to identify when the world was created. He used the dates given in the Bible (see table 1) of the pre-flood people (Adam, Enoch, Noah, etc.) to establish when Adam and Eve lived. Counting back so many years, plus 6 days, he discovered the date God had created the earth. He determined it was sometime in 4004 BCE. The Vice-Chancellor of the University of Cambridge, also looking to determine the date of creation, went one-step further. He fine-tuned the date and stated that the Earth was created on October 23, 4004 BCE, at 9 AM. It was a Sunday.

For hundreds of years people believed that creation happened in 4004 BCE. Discoveries in science tell us a different story. Today, most Westerners have let go of the 4004 BCE date. They reason... "How could such a recent date account for things such as trilobites, the dinosaurs and the action of plate tectonics?" It only took one hundred years for our societal viewpoint to change.

Date	Event	Earth Age
4004 BCE	Creation	0 yrs.
3874 BCE	Seth born when Adam was 130	130 yrs.
3769 BCE	Enos born when Seth was 105	235 yrs.
3679 BCE	Cainan born when Enos was 90	325 yrs
3609 BCE	Mahalaleen born when Cainan was 70	395 yrs.
3544 BCE	Jared born when Mahalaleen was 65	460 yrs.
3382 BCE	Enoch born when Jared was 162	622 yrs.
3317 BCE	Methuselah born when Enoch was 65	687 yrs.
3130 BCE	Lamech born when Methuselah was 187	874 yrs
2948 BCE	Noah born when Lamech was 182	1,056 yrs.
2446 BCE	Shem born when Noah was 502	1,558 yrs.
2348 BCE	Flood when Noah was 600	1,656 yrs.
2346 BCE	Arphaxad born when Shem was 100	1,658 yrs.
2311 BCE	Salah born when Arphad was 35	1,693 yrs.
2281 BCE	Eber born when Salah was 30	1,723 yrs.
2246 BCE	Peleg born when Eber was 34	1,758 yrs.
2217 BCE	Reu born when Peleg was 30	1,787 yrs.
2185 BCE	Serug born when Reu was 32	1,819 yrs.
2155 BCE	Nahor born when Serug was 30	1,849 yrs.
2126 BCE	Terah born when Nahor was 29	1,878 yrs.
1996 BCE	Abraham born when Terah was 139	2,008 yrs.
1921 BCE	Abraham enters Canaan at 75	2,083 yrs.

Table 1 - Bishop James Ussher's Dating Of Creation

If we want to understand where we came from we must be willing to look outside the box, or should I say, "The Book".

We continue to live entrenched in a cultural timeline that is incorrect - even with all of the recent discoveries in the sciences. The currently accepted timeline tells us that civilization began in Sumer around 4000 BCE. Supporters of this notion state that the pyramids in Egypt were built shortly thereafter. Archeologists, historians and researchers into our distant past want us to believe that humanity moved from living in caves and huts into a full-blown society nearly overnight.

Alternative historians, such as Brad Steiger, Michael Cremo, Graham Hancock, John Anthony West, Klaus Dona, Zecharia Sitchin and Eric Van Daniken, believe that evidence of our past is being hidden from us. At worst, new discoveries are not being discussed and mainstream researchers are overlooking important finds. The suppression of evidence keeps our history nice, neat, ordered and controlled. The exposure of newly acquired facts and information that do not conform to the norm would force us to look outside the box. For some, this is a very uncomfortable idea.

Recent archeological discoveries in Syria and Turkey are challenging contemporary mainstream archeologists. In Bosnia, a series of pyramid structures have been found. Called the Bosnian Pyramids, they have been dated, conservatively speaking, to 7000 BCE. In Turkey, a presumed religious structure filled with monolithic columns and detailed carvings, called Göbekli Tepe, has been dated to have been built around 9000 BCE. Have you heard about either of these sites in the media? Have there been any shows on the *Discovery Channel* or *History Channel* talking about these incredible finds? Thanks to the Internet, information about these amazing discoveries is slowly being revealed. The result of these discoveries could revolutionize our thoughts about history.

Our myths, legends and oral tradition provide us with an image of our ancient past. These tales tell of the lives and experiences of our ancestors. Dating the events, chronicled in these ancient tales, is difficult if not impossible. The date of

Noah's flood, for example, is lost to posterity. Stone carvings, which describe the flood, have been found in Sumer. The carvings by themselves do not help us determine the date of the flood. Scientists are obliged to date the evidence in hand: the carved tablet, the rock and other strata in which the carving was found. If, on the other hand, there was a reference to a known (dated) person, a place or thing found within the writing itself a reasonably close if not exact date could be determined. This, in most instances, is not the case. The writings, stories and myths we have inherited never sound like a modern newspaper. The tales never begin with "On Friday, December 21, 2012 ..." If only they did!

Many historians are quick to dismiss information that comes to us from ancient cultures. They state that primitive people, in order to explain their surroundings, invented these creative stories. Comments using this line of reasoning can be found in Pedro Sarmiento De Gamboa's book the *"History of the Incas"* written in 1572 CE.

This absurd fable of their creation is held by these barbarians and they affirm and believe it as if they had really seen it to happen and come to pass. – History of the Incas, Pedro Sarmiento De Gamboa

When anthropologists investigated the cosmology of the Dogon people, their peers quickly dismissed their findings. The Dogon are an ethnic group of people living in the Mali region of Africa. French anthropologists Marcel Griaule and Germain Dieterlen in the early 20th century studied these primitive people. Dogon priests, over time, revealed to the anthropologists many of their secret myths, lores and traditions.

Griaule and Dieterlen reported the advanced astronomical knowledge these people possessed. The Dogon people were aware of the rings of Saturn and the moons that surround Jupiter. The Dogon also claimed that Sirius, the brightest star in the night sky, had a companion star. The Dogon describe it as being very small, incredibly heavy and white in color. Today, astronomers call this secondary, binary star, Sirius B. Sirius B is not visible to the naked eye. It was first observed with a telescope in 1862.

Astronomers, such as the legendary Carl Sagan, dismissed the potential knowledge of the Dogon, suggesting that the priests of this primitive group must have encountered Westerners prior to Griaule and Dieterlen's investigation. The Dogon, according to Sagan, took this scientific information about Sirius's binary star and in the course of 60 years incorporated this new knowledge into their cultural mythology. This explanation, nevertheless, does not address the Sigui ceremony that has been performed by the Dogon people every 60 years since at least the 12th century that celebrates the renewal of the world.

Mythic epics such as the Hindu *Mahabharata* and the *Ramayana* are described as being ambitious tales of fiction, or should I say, science fiction. These stories are portrayed as a figment of someone's wild imagination. Homer's epic tales *The Iliad* and *The Odyssey* also fall into the category of fantasy. Homer's sagas provide detailed descriptions of the people, places and events that transpired during the war between the people of Troy and the Greeks, the Trojan War. These heroic tales apparently provided enough factual information that in the 1870's Heinrich Schliemann discovered the mythic city of Troy. This find changed our view of Homer's work forever. What was once believed to be a fairy tale, overnight became recognized as an important historical document.

If the events documented in *The Iliad* are shown to be based upon historical information, then why not others? If the Dogon knew about specific astronomical information of our solar system then how are we to say that other technical information from ancient sources is false or make believe? Is it possible that the myths and legends from around the world are accounts of what occurred in our past?

Another problem encountered when dealing with a culture's mythology is it was often recorded long after the event occurred. What little we do have is memorialized in stone, on papyrus and on wood. This has created problems for many scholars. For example, we recognize the books contained within the New Testament were not written right after Jesus' death. Stories of Jesus' life were memorized and then told and retold for years before pen was put to paper. It is theorized that at least 50 years went by after Jesus' death before his life and work were collected and documented. These books are touted as the one and true word of God, despite a 50 year delay in documenting the facts of the day.

Books of Jesus' life and teachings that fall outside the current Bible called the *Apocrypha* are not accepted in much the same way. Manuscripts such as the ones found in the Egyptian town of Nag Hammadi are believed to have been written some time during the 4th century AD. These books include the *Gospel of Thomas*, the *Gospel of Mary* and the *Book Of Secrets Of John*. Were the concepts depicted in these texts a part of the original teachings of Jesus' ministry? Religious scholars resoundingly say No!

The majority of the myths we have today were passed down through the generations verbally. It is assumed that these stories, over time, were changed, modified and, likely, corrupted. How do experts suggest the corruption took place? Have you ever played the telephone game as a child? Do you remember that game? A group of people sit in a circle. A phrase is given to one of the people who will then whisper the phrase into a neighbor's ear. The goal is to transmit the unchanged phrase around the circle successfully. More often than not, the phrase at the end of the circle rarely resembles the original one.

Why is it so hard for some to believe that a story could be so important to a culture that it lived through their oral tradition until it was finally "written in stone"? Passing information orally was an integral part of early cultural life. Individuals were specialized in learning, sharing and retelling mythic information long before the creation of the printing press. These specialists would transmit their stories in the form of song or lyrical verse. Early explorers to the New World were amazed at the native population's ability to recall word for word transactions of long past treaties. In fact, in some Amerindian cultures it was correct etiquette at their councils for each speaker to repeat verbatim every word of what all his predecessors had said.

The Talmud, the rabbinic writings that form the basis of Orthodox Judaism, records:

It happened with King Ptolemy, that he gathered seventy-two elders, and gathered them in seventy-two houses, and did not reveal to them the purpose for which he had gathered them, and he went in to visit each of them, one by one, and he said to them, "Write for me the Torah of Moshe your teacher." The Holy One, Who is Blessed, gave to the heart of each of them, one by one, wisdom, and all of them arrived at a single understanding. – Tractate Megillah

In short, they were each able to translate the entire Torah, verbatim.

We no longer have the need to memorize and recall vast quantities of information. We open a book or turn on our computers to get the answers to our questions. We can typically store bits of information in our memory, but in our daily lives this is not a skill we practice anymore. We all do find that our recall ability works fine if we hear the same information repeated consistently. Christmas carols are a great example. These songs are only sung during a specific time of the year. Now granted, today many of us do not know the second verse to most Christmas carols; yet it is easy for Christians and non-Christians alike to sing along at least to the chorus of *Jingle Bells* or *Rudolf The Red Nose Reindeer*. Likewise, I will bet many readers will still be able to recall the opening tune to the epic voyage of Gilligan. Now think. How long was Gilligan supposed to be at sea? What happened to him and his boat? Who was on the boat with him? The same holds true when we ask the question what is the jingle describing the content of a Mc Donald's Big Mac sandwich?

We can take this concept one-step farther. Individuals who work as professional singers memorize vast amounts of music as part of their work. Think about the opera singer who learns all of the words to *Rigoletto* or *Madam Butterfly* or the local cover band who can play countless songs upon request. These requests might run the gamut from rock and roll to country or pop. Are they so unlike the bard who was raised listening to the local myths and legends and was later able to tell these tales to an awaiting crowd? Could mythical information be passed reasonably intact? We think so! Especially if what they were conveying was important to them. As you will discover, the tales of our past are anything but boring.

Current convention indicates that each culture's myths and legends developed independently. This belief becomes problematic when you evaluate cultures worldwide. Scientists state the Sumerians were the first group to develop a full-blown culture. They flourished about 6,000 years ago in Iraq. The Sumerians preceded the Babylonians, a group of Biblical fame. It only seems logical that their story of creation, the flood, giants, and a warring race of gods would filter out and influence the cultures of the neighboring areas such as Egypt, Italy and Greece. These cultures are in relatively close proximity to Sumer and each other. Trade between these divergent groups could account for a merging of traditions and beliefs. This could lead to sharing and borrowing stories from one another.

There is one teeny-tiny little problem when you try to assert that different cultures came up with their own unique stories. Mythological traditions found worldwide are remarkably similar to each other. If we were speaking strictly about the mythology found in Eurasia, it could reasonably be deduced that the stories spread from a singular source. Granted the names may have changed and specific details may be different, but the essence of the stories is virtually identical.

One has to stop and rethink what is going on when you include the mythology of North and South America and especially Australia into the mix. It insists you to take a step back and look at it with fresh eyes. The prevailing theory states that the Americas were first settled around 12,000 BCE. Australia, amazingly, is believed to have been first populated over 40,000 years ago. These dates, to some, may seem extremely conservative but they still serve to support the point. The myths found in these geographically diverse locations and cultures surprisingly follow the same story line to those told in Eurasia, including the ones found in the Bible.

One other concern when talking about oral traditions is the contamination of an indigenous culture's cosmology with Christianity. The cosmology of a culture relates to the religious and philosophical systems of that group. It seeks to explain the nature of reality and the meaning of their existence. In the Americas and elsewhere around the world, we find instances where the native people have incorporated aspects of Christianity into their worldview. We have made a vigorous effort to sort those stories out. Fortunately for us the missionaries who came to the new world documented the unbelievable history of these people. Reports made by individuals like Polo de Ondegardo of the native people's beliefs, can make one realize that the stories of the native populations he records were a genuine part of their cosmology.

According to the most certain and true opinion there could not have been inhabitants in this land before the universal deluge; for as it is certain that all men sprang from our father Adam, and that in the period between Adam and Noah so wide a dispersion could not have taken place, how is it possible that these Indians can have had any knowledge of the deluge?...

It is certain that there were no inhabitants in this land until many days and years after the deluge: for it was necessary that the descendants of those who were saved in the ark should spread themselves to the new world, and it is certain that they cannot have handed down these fables to their sons. – Narratives Of The Rites And Laws Of The Yncas, Polo de Ondegardo

The format this book will take is simple. Its focus is on our most ancient of stories. It follows the text and chronology laid out by the myths themselves. Since we are attempting to expand our understanding of our past, then using the Biblical texts as a guideline is a logical place to begin. Why focus on these stories? Because these are the ones we in the Western world are familiar. We will be adding into and comparing these texts not only to current scientific discoveries, but also to the myths and legends from other ancient cultures from around the world. In doing so, a more complete understanding of our past can be derived. Each story contains a piece of evidence, a breadcrumb or specific detail that collectively fills in many particulars of our past and provides a bigger broader picture of ourselves.

We have made a sincere effort to report what is known, and we have attempted to put together a congruent theory of our past. Some of what will be discussed is speculative on our part. Parts are assertions and educated guesses. Do we know all the facts? Probably not. We have compiled our findings to inform you of what is known or was generally accepted as truth in the past versus the prepackaged malarkey that has been instilled in us today.

Be prepared... Many of the concepts presented in this book differ from those widely held in the Western world. Could it be possible that the writers, chroniclers and scribes of our distant past actually recorded a realistic view of our origin? Give yourself the opportunity to be like one of these discoverers and step outside the box. Open your heart and mind to what you will read. If it makes sense and is plausible, keep it. If what is being discussed sounds like a bunch of hooey, then let it go. Read on and decide for yourself. We believe that once you start looking at what was held as truth in the past, you will at least go Hmmmmm...

In The Beginning...

Nearly every culture around the world has a creation story. To begin our journey into our past we need to define the word "God", the great universal creator. Humanity's deepest underlying concept of God is the same regardless of the name associated with this presence. Generally, God has been used to describe the energy, the force, the being, the consciousness that existed prior to our creation. This God caused our world to come into existence. This God underscores everything in our universe.

Most will agree that human beings cannot fully understand the true nature of God. We often imagine God as a person. Many of us have given God a sex making him easier to describe. Is he physical, vibrational, energetic or pure consciousness? Ultimately, we are only able to grasp a small portion of whom or what God truly is. He is beyond our comprehension. Our limited mental capabilities make it impossible to fathom what it means to be infinite with infinite knowledge, powers and abilities. The vastness of what we call God is everything combined into one and at the same time nothing. As such, we can only know God through his qualities and attributes. The list below is a small sampling of a few of the qualities and attributes generally associated with our perception of God.

- God is beyond the reach of our senses, mind and intellect
- God is eternal, meaning he had no beginning or end
- God is omnipotent and all-powerful
- God is our Creator and we are a part of His creation
- He is present everywhere

- He is everything and nothing
- God is the consciousness that pervades our universe
- God is the one who, through his unseen laws, supports, sustains and governs the Universe

The authors recognize that defining God as viewed by every cult, religion or non-religion is an impossible task. An atheist would argue there is no God. Primitive cultures from around the world have deep-set beliefs in an omnipotent God. Early chronologist, historians and missionaries traveled to the Americas and could not accept the Native American's notion of a supreme being. How could the God of these "savages" be the same as the one and true God of Christianity? Based upon the cosmology of these native people it is evident they had a clear understanding of the difference between the God that underlies all of creation and the gods you will be hearing more about in this book.

This book contains references to a great Creator called "God" as well as other beings that humankind saw as gods.

We will be referring to the creator God, as Giorgio Tsoukalos the publisher of Legendary Times Magazine likes to say, with a capitol "G" - God. Other gods, whom we will be meeting later in the book, will be referenced with a small "g" - god. As we move forward, we will quickly be separating God from god and you will see evidence that the two are not one in the same.

The only exception to this rule is when we are discussing the god of the Bible. We will be using the name God, with a capitol "G" to denote God as the proper name of a specific individual. This is not to be confused with the creator God. This god (God) is the god who lived in the heavens, walked the Earth and interacted with humankind. For clarity sake, we will also be referring to God, both big and small "g's", in the masculine tense for ease of reading.

The story of creation most Westerners share is the one depicted in the first book of the Bible, Genesis. For centuries, the words printed within the Bible were taken verbatim... God created the earth, plants, animals and man in six Earth days.

28

Contemporary scientists, based upon astronomical, archeological and cosmological discoveries, describe this story as a simplistic over-exaggeration of how we came into being. They support their claim by informing us that primitives who lack any kind of historical or scientific credibility wrote it. Could the biblical story of creation provide us with a cogent description of our past?

Theologians seem content with the new scientific theories of our origin that have been published in the last 200 years. Concepts such as the Big Bang theory, planetary formation and the development of life on Earth do not contradict their fundamental views. They have chosen to step outside the box and accept some of the possibilities that science provides regarding our origin. As for the rest of us, we have followed suit and now believe that creation did not take place in six days as the Bible says, but instead took billions of years to complete. These scientific discoveries, while providing us with a clearer picture of our past, did one other thing. They caused many of us to throw the biblical creation myth away right along with the belief that the world was flat.

Does the Bible provide us with a relatively realistic, although significantly abbreviated history of our past, when viewed through the eyes of science? Like Genesis 1:1 we will be starting "in the beginning" and looking at what the Bible says about our origin. Genesis 1:1 states:

In the beginning, God created the heaven and the Earth. - Genesis 1:1

The most common interpretation of this statement is "*God created the heaven and the Earth.*" Period! From nothingness, the heavens and the Earth came into existence. Nothing preceded their appearance and like a magician with his magic wand, they miraculously appeared. If one were to interpret this statement in a slightly different light, the narrative of the entire story changes. Consider if you will... What if the statement "*God created the heavens and the earth*" refers not to the act of creation, but instead is simply an introduction to the story that is to follow. Once introduced, the author then elaborates and provides a detailed description of how this process took place.

If the opening line of the book of Genesis is simply an introduction to what will follow, then the story of creation does not begin until the next passage, Genesis 1:2. We find some amazing similarities between this new opening line when it is compared to the creation myths from other cultures.

Genesis 1:2: *Now the earth proved to be formless and waste and there was darkness upon the surface of [the] watery deep; and God's active force was moving to and fro over the surface of the waters.*

Egyptian Creation Myth: *In the beginning, before there was any land of Egypt, all was darkness, and there was nothing but a great waste of water called Nun.*

Japanese Creation Myth: *Before the heavens and the earth came into existence, all was a chaos, unimaginably limitless and without definite shape or form.* - Deity-of-the-August-Center-of-Heaven

Mesopotamian/Babylonian Creation Myth: *When on high the heaven had not been named, Firm ground below had not been called by name, When primordial Apsu, their begetter, And Mummu-Tiamat, she who bore them all, Their waters mingled as a single body.* - Enuma Elish

Hindu Creation Myth: *There was neither day nor night, nor sky nor earth, nor darkness nor light, nor any other thing, save only One, unapprehensible by intellect... Darkness there was: at first concealed in darkness this All was indiscriminated chaos. All that existed then was void and form less.* - Vishnu Purana

Slavic Creation Myth: *In the beginning, there were no earth and no people, only the primordial sea. Bielobog flew over the face of the waters in the shape of a swan and was lonely.* - Based on Bulgarian and Ukrainian sources

Boshongo Creation Myth: *In the beginning, there was only darkness, water, and the great god Bumba.* - Bantu tribe of Central Africa

The chances of similar myths within relatively close geographical areas to one another are possible, even likely to occur. The rub comes when you cross the ocean and encounter myths such as those held by the aborigines of Australia, the Maya and Aztec of South America and traditional Native American cultures such as the Hopi.

Arente (Central Australia) Creation Myth: *Before the World came into existence, there was a mass of dark and formless matter, a vast watery expanse or a somewhat featureless plain. Spiritual Ancestors defines all spaces and all time out of what was potentially there in this dark, nameless matter, 'ngallala yawun', everything soft like jelly.*

Mayan Creation Myth: *At the time (before creation), there were no people, no animals, no trees, no rocks, or anything. All was a wasteland, desolate and limitless. Above the inert flatness, space lay immobile, while above the chaos, the motionless immensity of the sea was resting. There was neither structure nor activity. What was below was unlike what was above, not one thing as seen standing. Only the deaf calmness of the waters was felt, which seemed to be precipitated into the abyss.* - The Popol Vuh

Aztec Creation Myth: *The Aztecs believe that in the beginning of the world, there was nothing but darkness. One great god*

named Ometeotl watched over this darkness in complete solitude. - The Dawn and Dusk of Man

Hopi Creation Myth: *The world at first was endless space in which existed only the creator, Taiowa. This world had not time, no shape and no life, except in the mind of the Creator.* - Creation Stories From Around The World

Taken in total, the myths seem to indicate that the Earth and our universe were in an unmanifest state at this point in creation. We can only imagine it as an energy filled with potential. This potential energy is a single aspect of God. Lynn Buess (Buess, 1978) describes creation as *"The desire for movement within the existence of the unmanifest eventually topples the homeostasis and we have the beginning of creation and manifestation."* These concepts, although vague, attempt to describe what was happening prior to the act of creation.

Another concept is introduced in the Bible, the idea of vibration being used as a mechanism of creation. In the most famous quote from the Bible, in Genesis 1:3, we learn:

And God said, "Let there be light," and there was light. - Genesis 1:3

If you read further through the Bible's creation story, the words *"And God said..."*, or some version of these words, are used over and over again immediately before each act of creation. This concept of words existing before creation is reiterated in the New Testament book of John: *"In the beginning was the Word, and the Word was with God, and the Word was God."* - John 1:1.

When we say a name, when we utter a word, we are sending sound vibrations out into the world. In its simplest form, the spoken word manifests as an acoustic vibration, this is transmitted via sound waves. A sound wave is a longitudinal mechanical wave of a given frequency. Sound energy is sent out through air or other material by the oscillation of its mechanical waves. The sounds we hear are made up of sound waves that are broadcasted at frequencies within the range of human hearing.

We describe other features within our world in similar ways. Take the electromagnetic spectrum. The electromagnetic spectrum is made up of seven different frequency ranges of radiation. It includes radio waves, microwaves, infrared radiation, visible radiation (light), ultraviolet light, x-rays and gamma rays. The electromagnetic spectrum is described in terms of its wavelength. Radio frequencies vibrate at the slowest, lowest frequency while gamma rays vibrate the fastest. The light and colors we see in our world fall somewhere in the middle of this spectrum of radiation.

While sound energy is not considered part of the electromagnetic spectrum, sound waves can be expressed in terms of color or electromagnetic radiation. For example, the frequency of the note "middle C" is 262 Hz. If you go up 41 octaves above middle C, you reach the frequency vibration of the color green. We do not yet know how far above or below the note middle C we can go in either direction. Most frequencies exist outside our normal range of perception. We are only able to observe a very small portion of the vibrations that fill our world, namely colors and sounds.

According to string theory, absolutely everything in the universe, both matter and forces, items seen and unseen are all comprised of tiny vibrating strings. String theory developed out the study of particle physics. Particle physicists study elementary subatomic particles including protons, neutrons, electrons, photons, quarks, neutrinos, muons and a wide range of exotic particles. Their goal is to understand the principals and relationship between the physical matter and radiation that fill our world. String theory, in turn, looks to find a common explanation for the fundamental particles that make up our world and the four main forces in nature. These forces are the strong and weak nuclear forces, electromagnetism and gravity.

Unlike classical physics which states that the universe is made up of small static and unchanging 3-dimensional particles (atoms and subatomic particles), string theorists assert that a particle is really a 1-dimensional vibrating, oscillating string. Think of these strings as being like the string on a guitar. Different musical notes can be created depending on the size, tension and how a guitar string is plucked. It is believed by string theorists that the vibration of these strings is what underscores the formation of all matter and radiation in our world. The difference between one particle and another is its resonant pattern or how it vibrates. One resonant pattern makes it a photon, while another produces a heavy particle found within the nucleus of an atom. Simply put, some vibrations produce matter while others make energy. A low frequency allows dense matter to form, while a higher frequency creates less dense matter that is more refined.

Light, sound, mountains and even each of us are all the same. The only thing that differs is the nature and complexity of our make-up as defined by our specific vibration. This is also true for every thought, belief, feeling and intention we have. They are made up of vibrations, vibrations that play an integral part and create the fabric of the world in which we live. With God setting the vibration for the creation of our universe, we can now explore the act of creation itself.

It was once believed that our universe was infinite. It had no beginning and no end. It was not expanding, nor contracting. Its size was so massive that it extended out into space to a size that boggled the mind and then some. The model for a static universe was supported by Albert Einstein's theory of relativity. Willem de Sitter, working the theory of relativity, showed that Einstein's theory could also describe a universe that was expanding in size. The scientific community of the day agreed that the principles of an expanding universe were sound, but there was not any observational evidence to support de Sitter's claims.

This all changed in 1929 when Edwin Hubble discovered that distant galaxies were moving away from us (our vantage point). Instead of being static, our universe was indeed growing, and growing at incredible speeds. Monsignor Georges Lemaître, a Catholic priest and physicist, in 1933, derived a simple (mathematically speaking) solution to this problem, which explained the expanding universe. Using his calculations, he projected the expansion of the universe back in time and suggested that at one time our universe existed as a central point and then expanded outward. He believed that the universe, instead of being static, was created from a "primeval atom" which increased in size over time. He describes the expansion of this primeval atom as "*the Cosmic Egg exploding at the moment of creation*". Today, the theory that our universe originated from a central point is known as the "Big Bang Theory".

The Big Bang theory tells us that our universe was created 13.7 billion years ago. This date, however, is based upon how far we can see into space. We cannot see the edges of the universe. The farthest light we can detect comes to us from stars and galaxies 13.7 billion light years away. Our limited ability to look farther out into space has led scientist to make errant claims about the size and age of our universe. How big and how old the universe is, remains a mystery.

Scientists do agree, based upon prevailing knowledge, that all matter and energy was contained in a single small point, a singularity. Some speculate it was the size of a dime, others a walnut. This point was made of densely packed matter and energy. Then, for whatever reason, and one in which scientists cannot explain, BANG! As fast, or perhaps faster, than the speed of light, the densely packed matter and energy that made up this point began to expand.

Forces that rule our world such as electromagnetism, gravitation, weak and strong interactions are believed to be present within microseconds seconds (10^{-43} seconds) after the explosion. Subatomic particles such as quarks, hadrons and leptons appeared as the universe continued to expand and cool. All of the energy, during these early moments, was in the form of radiation and not matter as we know it. By the time 10 seconds had elapsed, the universe was filled with photons. A photon is a basic unit of electromagnetic energy, namely light.

According to Molly Read of the Observational Cosmology Group, "*The universe was still really hot, so hot that ordinary atoms couldn't even exist. Electrons caused very small packets of light called photons to scatter continuously, and if you can believe it, light was actually linked, or coupled, to the particles, causing the whole universe to glow. This is the stage that scientists like to call the primordial soup because the universe looked like a plasma "soup" of protons, electrons, neutrons, neutrinos, photons, etc."*

Can the passage from Genesis 1:3 be interpreted literally? *"And God said "Let there be light" and there was light."* This "light" lasted for 380,000 years until the universe had cooled down enough for atoms such as hydrogen and helium to form. The story of creation does not end there. The first day of creation continues in Genesis 1:4 - 5:

...and God brought about a division between the light and the darkness. And God began calling the light Day, but the darkness he called Night. - Genesis 1:4 - 5

For many, this phrase is very confusing. It is assumed that the cycles of day and night, (the rotation of the Earth around the sun on its axis) is what is being described. We have one little problem... the Earth had not yet been formed. What could the ancient writers be describing in Genesis if not days and nights on our planet?

The Big Bang theory tells us that our universe is still expanding. Astronomers, evaluating the structure of galaxies, were having a hard time figuring out why galaxies were not stretching or being pulled apart as our universe expands. The only solution to this perplexing problem was gravity. They believed gravity was the glue that held galaxies together. Unfortunately, based upon the parts of each galaxy that can be seen, it was deduced that there is not enough mass, not enough "stuff" in a galaxy to account for its gravitational anomalies. So what is holding galaxies together? The answer according to some theorists is "dark matter".

Swiss astronomer Fritz Zwicky first popularized the concept of dark matter in 1934. Zwicky alleged it accounted for the missing mass he detected when studying the orbital velocities of galaxies. Scientists are unsure of the composition of dark matter. Some speculate that it is composed of elementary particles that neither emit nor reflect electromagnetic radiation, thus making it "dark" to the observer. According to an article in Science Daily (Durham University 2007) *"Even though little is known about their nature, evidence for the presence of dark matter is overwhelming, from observations of galaxies, to clusters of galaxies, to the Universe as a whole."* Cosmologists agree that dark matter not only contributes to more than 90% of our known universe, but that the evolution, structure and formation of galaxies is directly related to its gravitational forces.

Is the Bible, when it talks about the separation of light and darkness, actually describing the formation of observable matter verses dark matter? It is after the formation of matter in the universe that Genesis 1:5 continues:

And there came to be evening and there came to be morning, a first day. - Genesis 1:5

Have we just ended an epoch of cosmic evolution in biblical terms? Scientists at Tufts University seem to think so. They refer to the development of the early universe as Epoch 1, Particulate Evolution. Genesis 1:6 - 7 goes on to tell us:

And God went on to say: "Let an expanse come to be in between the waters and let a dividing occur between the waters and the waters." Then God proceeded to make the expanse and to make a division between the waters that should be beneath the expanse and the waters that should be above the expanse. And it came to be so. - Genesis 1:6 - 7

The next phase in cosmic evolution, Epoch 2, according to cosmologists was the development of galaxies. The universe was homogeneous until this point. It was a sea of photons and early forms of hydrogen, helium and dark matter. The cosmos continued to cool and the building blocks of our universe began to condense. These elementary particles, through their gravitational pull, began clumping together, leaving vast areas of empty space between them. These clumps of matter and dark matter over time consolidated to form the galaxies. The epoch ends and so does the second day.

And God began to call the expanse Heaven. And there came to be evening and there came to be morning, a second day.
- Genesis 1:8

Events move quickly as we enter the 3rd day of creation. In Genesis 1:9 - 10 we are told:

And God went on to say: "Let the waters under the heavens be brought together into one place and let the dry land appear." And it came to be so. And God began calling the dry land Earth, but the bringing together of the waters he called Seas. Further, God saw that [it was] good. - Genesis 1:9 - 10

In Epoch 3 of our cosmic evolution, stars that fill the galaxies begin to take shape. Stars form as local gasses and dust are drawn together through their gravitational forces. As their mass and gravity increased, the molecular cloud from which they were formed collapsed causing their temperatures to rise. Eventually nuclear fusion began. These solar bodies were able to give off light and heat once ignited. The remaining clouds of gas and dust that surrounded the stars also aggregated. Planets such as the ones found in our solar system are formed. The formation of planets begins and ends our cosmic evolution as well as Epoch 4.

The formation of the Earth also moves us from a cosmic timeline into the local timeline of our planet. Scientifically speaking, we are entering into the earliest history of the Earth, the Precambrian period. It is hard to imagine the birth of the Earth some 4.5 billion years ago. The Earth was still a molten mass of rock during the earliest stages of the Precambrian. As it cooled, heavier elements such as iron sank to the core of the planet, while lighter ones rose to the surface. Volcanic activity across the planet emitted gases such as ammonia, hydrogen, carbon dioxide, methane and water vapor. This developed into a dense gas cloud zone, which could be likened to an early atmosphere. The density of these early burning vapors caused the surface of the Earth to lie shrouded in darkness.

It is also during this early phase of the Earth's development that the Moon formed. It is theorized that a planet the size of Mars struck the Earth. This impact caused a large amount of matter to be ejected into space. This matter formed a disk, similar to Saturn's rings, around the Earth. The ejected matter eventually condensed forming the Moon.

Water, as rainfall, condensed as temperatures continued cooling. The heavy, dense cloud cover that surrounded the Earth produced violent storms. Oceans began to form around 4.4 billion years ago even though the surface temperature of the planet was still around 446° F.

The first signs of life, according to the fossil record, appeared on Earth around 3.8 billion years ago. The Earth's atmosphere was filled with toxic gases. Simple forms of bacteria were found thriving amid this sea of toxicity,. The earliest microorganisms discovered on Earth, called chemoautotrophs, were anaerobic, that is they did not utilize oxygen for metabolism like we do. They derived their energy from the intake of inorganic substances such as hydrogen sulfide, sulfur and ammonia and produced oxygen as a by-product. This kind of bacteria is still found on the Earth living in some of the most hostile environments on the planet.

Life continued to evolve on Earth. Organisms known as "eukaryotic" cells, which included some of the earliest plant, fungal and animal life, appeared as early as 1.8 billion years ago. Eukaryotes are organisms that have a cellular nucleus. The nucleus contains the cell's genetic materials.

The middle of the Precambrian presented increased oxygen levels on the planet. This caused the extinction of many forms of bacteria but supported an explosion of eukaryote life. By the end of the Precambrian, worm-like Parmia and Sinosabellidites appeared in the fossil record. The earliest fossils of trilobites and archeocyathids (a kind of sponge) are also found. These early plants and animals lived in the water. This is an important concept as we move forward.

The next era, the Paleozoic, saw an explosion of life forms. The Paleozoic started about 542 million years ago and ended 251 million years ago. This era is represented by the development of animals with shells and exoskeletons, such as trilobites, brachiopods and mollusks and sea plants. By the middle of this period, fish and cephalopoda (octopi, squid and cuttlefish) are swimming in the ocean. Primitive plants had begun to move onto land. Not long after insects, including anthropoids and arachnids took up residence. By the end of the Paleozoic Era, huge forests filled with giant insects cover the land. Tetrapods (vertebrate animals having four limbs) and amphibians left the water and began evolving by the edge of the sea. As this era closes, the first reptiles joined the ranks of animal life on land.

The development of life on land is reflected in the biblical quote of the later part of the 3rd day:

And God went on to say: "Let the earth cause grass to shoot forth, vegetation bearing seed, fruit trees yielding fruit according to their kinds, the seed of which is in it, upon the earth." And it came to be so. And the earth began to put forth grass, vegetation bearing seed according to its kind and trees yielding fruit, the seed of which is in it according to its kind. Then God saw that [it was] good. - Genesis 1:11 - 12

We have proposed earlier that the ancient writers of the Bible were knowledgeable of the evolution of the universe and its major periods of development. During the first day, the universe was created via the Big Bang. This day ended with the formation of matter and particles within the universe. Day two was characterized by the formation of stars and galaxies including our own. Day three was a very busy day for God. He formed our planet and created life. Life started out as single celled organisms and concluded with plant life and insects ruling the Earth. There was a small assortment of amphibians and reptiles found during this period, but the numbers were nominal. Another period ends...

And there came to be evening and there came to be morning, a third day. - Genesis 1:13

The "Great Dying" of life on Earth marks the end of the Paleozoic Era and the third day. The Permian-Triassic Extinction was the most severe extinction event ever experienced on the Earth. The first of many mass extinction events, the Permian-Triassic Extinction occurred 251.4 million years ago. Ninety-six percent of all marine species, 70% of vertebrate land animals and over 50% of the insect species perished.

There are a couple of theories as to what happened. The most prevalent theory is associated with the eruption of a super volcano in Siberia (the Siberian Traps) at approximately the same time. The volcano emitted a plume of ash and hydrocarbons into the atmosphere for approximately 200,000 years. Gas and ash filled the Earth's atmosphere blocking sunlight from passing through and caused global temperatures to plummet.

Another theory as to the demise of the early life on Earth was the discovery of a giant impact crater found in the Wilkes Land region of Antarctica. This 300-mile wide crater suggests that a meteor, perhaps six times the size of the one that hit the Earth and killed off the dinosaurs, struck the Earth about 250 million years ago. The impact is thought to have been so massive that it contributed to the breaking up of the supercontinent Gondwana. Could this impact event set off the super volcano in Siberia? It is hard to say. As for the 90% of life that died off on the planet, their day certainly did come to an end...

Of all the sections of the biblical creation story, this next verse has been the most difficult to decipher.

And God went on to say: "Let luminaries come to be in the expanse of the heavens to make a division between the day and the night; and they must serve as signs and for seasons and for days and years. And they must serve as luminaries in the expanse of the heavens to shine upon the earth." And it came to be so. And God proceeded to make the two great luminaries, the greater luminary for dominating the day and the lesser luminary for dominating the night, and also the stars. Thus God put them in the expanse of the heavens to shine upon the earth, and to dominate by day and by night and to make a division between the light and the darkness. Then God saw that [it was] good. And there came to be evening and there came to be morning, a fourth day.
Genesis 1:14 - 19

God, in this section, is said to create the sun, moon and stars. This act of creation, based upon prevailing science, should have occurred millions if not billions of years earlier. The appearance of the sun prior to this point in time is supported by the fact that plant life exploded during the Paleozoic Era. Plant life requires light energy, as in solar radiation, to support photosynthesis. Photosynthesis is the process by which plants utilize sunlight to produce the fuels they need to live. No sunlight, no plants. Pretty simple.

So why did the ancient writers place the appearance of the sun, moon and stars so late in the story? One thought is that this passage was moved from a different location. Perhaps this section of the creation story was originally the third day of creation as opposed to the fourth day. This certainly would fit nicely within our timeline.

If this was not the case, we have come up with a theory, which may explain this apparent discrepancy. Until very late in the Paleozoic Era, the bulk of all animal life was found in the depths of the oceans. Plant life, by the end of the era, had taken off covering the land. The fossil record indicates that amphibians and early reptiles appear very late in this period. Their small numbers do not account for the bulk of terrestrial life.

Then disaster strikes. A giant meteor hits Antarctica setting off a super volcano in Siberia. The dust and ash expelled shrouds the Earth in darkness for a few hundred thousand years. Slowly life on Earth began to rebound and as you will see, life moved from the depths of the oceans to life on land. Could this biblical passage be indicating the change from life under the waters to life beneath the sun, moon and stars?

Our tale of creation continues. The fifth day of the biblical story begins. So does the next era, the Mesozoic. Life on earth during this period is about to see some big changes. The Mesozoic era is best known as the "Age of Dinosaurs". We see the rise of dinosaurs on land. Giant creatures inhabit the seas. Pterosaur, or as they are better known - pterodactyl, take flight and fill the air. This next step in evolution is clearly described in Genesis 1:20 - 23.

And God went on to say: "Let the waters swarm forth a swarm of living souls and let flying creatures fly over the earth upon the face of the expanse of the heavens." And God proceeded to create the great sea monsters and every living soul that moves about, which the waters swarmed forth according to their kinds, and every winged flying creature according to its kind. And God got to see that [it was] good. With that God blessed them, saying: "Be fruitful and become many and fill the waters in the sea basins, and let the flying creatures become many in the earth. - Genesis 1:20 - 23

If you compare this passage to the opening of the 6th day as presented in the bible, it is easy to see why we have identified this quotation as describing the Mesozoic era.

And God went on to say: "Let the earth put forth living souls according to their kinds, domestic animal and moving animal and wild beast of the earth according to its kind." And it came to be so. And God proceeded to make the wild beast of the earth according to its kind and the domestic animal according to its kind and every moving animal of the ground according to its kind. And God got to see that [it was] good. - Genesis 1:24 - 25

On the 5th day (Genesis 1:20 - 23), the writers refer to the diversity of life forms on Earth as monsters and creatures. We have flying creatures filling the air and sea monsters swimming in the waters. Granted, they did not say, dinosaurs walked the Earth, but as you may recall, reptiles and amphibians existed prior to and survived the Permian-Triassic extinction event. During this era, however, giant sea animals (monsters?) such as ichthyosaurs and plesiosaur make their first appearance. The same holds true for the pterosaurs. It is in this period that "winged creatures" took flight. In stark contrast, on the 6th day of the creation story (Genesis 1:24 - 25), the newly evolving animal life is not referred to as "creatures", but instead as animals (domestic or otherwise) and wild beasts. Quite a different image from what we see in Genesis 1:20 - 23.

Like the fourth day, the fifth day comes to a tragic end as well. Researchers could not identify the cause of the dinosaurs' demise for years. This extinction event is known as the Cretaceous-Tertiary Extinction or the K-T event. They knew something dramatic had occurred to hasten the downfall of the dinosaurs but could not pinpoint the exact event. Theories, both practical and absurd abound.

The year 1980 produced a breakthrough in helping to solve this mystery. A team of researchers discovered a distinct layer of sedimentary materials that was composed of extraordinary amounts of the metal iridium. This layer of material separated the time when dinosaurs roamed the Earth from the next period, where they were no longer found.

The currently accepted cause for the demise of the dinosaurs is a meteor/asteroid that impacted the Earth 65.5 million years ago near Chicxulub in the Yucatán Peninsula. This meteor left a dispersal pattern of iridium circling the entire planet. This is what helped researchers locate the position of the impact. Another theory, which may explain the end of the dinosaurs' reign, is the discovery of a gigantic volcanic eruption, which was centered in west India - the Deccan Traps. There is strong evidence of volcanic activity when looking at samples of material that lies within the K-T boundary. Asteroid impact, volcanic activity or both, the result was the same. Seventy percent of land animals and 95% of sea animals disappeared from the face of the planet.

And there came to be evening and there came to be morning, a fifth day. - Genesis 1:23

The sixth day, from a biblical point of view is straightforward. God creates the animals that inhabit the Earth and in a final act of creation, he creates man.

And God went on to say: "Let us make man in our image, according to our likeness, and let them have in subjection the fish of the sea and the flying creatures of the heavens and the domestic animals and all the earth and every moving animal that is moving upon the earth." And God proceeded to create the man in his image, in God's image he created him; male and female he created them. Further, God blessed them and God said to them: "Be fruitful and become many and fill the earth and subdue it, and have in subjection the fish of the sea and the flying creatures of the heavens and every living creature that is moving upon the earth. - Genesis 1:26 - 29

Historically speaking, the Mesozoic Era gave way to the Cenozoic Era 65 million years ago. The Cenozoic Era is sometimes referred to as the "Age of Mammals". Small mammals existed during the Mesozoic Era, but their physical size and population were minute. The Cenozoic saw a change to all of that. With the dinosaurs out of the way, mammals were able to thrive. Small mammals such as rodents and small horses are common early in this era. Early elephants and rhinoceroses' appear on land. Whales, the first marine mammals, bound in the sea. Nearing the end of this era, modern animals such as cattle, sheep, goats, antelope and gazelle are also common. It is during the later part of the Cenozoic Era that the first hominids, the precursor to modern man make their appearance.

We are going to end our investigation into the biblical story of creation here with the creation of man. Before we go, we would like to leave you with these words:

After that God saw everything he had made and, look! [it was] very good. And there came to be evening and there came to be morning, a sixth day. - Genesis 1:31

A God By Any Other Name

In the last chapter we explored the Judeo-Christian story of Creation and compared it to current scientific theories about the formation of our universe, our world and ourselves. The limiting belief in a single all-encompassing god (other than during the brief reign of the Egyptian god/king Akhenaten) can only be found in the Judeo-Christian spiritual and cultural tradition. The conviction to the existence of a singular, kind and benevolent deity does not pervade any other culture on the Earth. Andrew Lang (Lang, 1913) states, *"It may be argued that a belief in a Creator is itself a myth"*. It does not explain, according to Lang, the attitude of awe and moral obedience we feel in relationship to a supposedly fictitious God. He goes on to question, why after having a belief in a Creator God did humanity go on to develop such wild and scandalous stories about him?

Could the events recorded in the mythology of other cultures provide a realistic representation of our past similar to what we discovered when we reviewed the texts found in the Bible? What if in our travels back in time we find ourselves in a place that seems more like science fiction than fact?

Mythology tells us that multiple gods, each with their own unique and distinct personalities, lived in our past. The gods are portrayed as having taken physical form. The gods, excluding the omnipotent Creator God, were seen as immortal beings, with lifetimes that extended far longer than our own. It is also clear from the texts that they could die or be killed. Early accounts tell of gods who actively participated in the formation of the Earth and development of humankind. They could be seen, heard, felt and touched. It also seems apparent from their accounts that the gods did not exist solely on the etheric realm but spent time on Earth. This was especially true prior to the great flood as reported in the Bible, the flood Noah survived.

Our mythology is filled with stories of torrid romances, elaborate and intricate plots, violence, scandals and conspiracies. Their story, instead of being the peaceful creation of our world and humankind as is portrayed in the Bible, is filled with wars between the gods. The gods were envisioned as being notoriously cruel to each other and their behavior towards humankind was not much better. Rivalry between them was rampant. The gods are often described as fighting with each other, vying for ultimate power and control.

The gods are also reported as being able to do amazing things. They had what we now know as technology that far exceeded our ancestors. They had vehicles that are described as celestial chariots, cars or planes. They could take to the skies and fly over vast distances in these vehicles. They had astonishing weapons that could smote their enemies and cause devastation to the land. The gods could also change their appearance and take on the form of both man and beast. There are even stories of the gods assuming the identity of another god in order to carry out their usually ill intentioned plans.

This is something that bothered Lang. He could not figure out how such a wide distribution of these absurd, yet remarkably similar stories and traditions could have occurred. He wondered if they developed independently in each culture or if they were somehow carried from one culture to another.

Bits and pieces of our history can be found globally in mythology. Deciphering who is who, or what the truth is, can be likened to putting together a giant jigsaw puzzle where the pieces of several puzzles were tossed into one box. We strive to put the puzzle together but quickly discover the content of the box does not match the picture on the top. We tirelessly endeavor to put the pieces together so they look like the image on the cover with no success. Frustrated, we wonder why the pieces just do not seem to fit together correctly. Likewise, our present understanding of our history does not fit the evidence in hand. We have many of the pieces but they do not match what we understand to be true.

It is uncanny that our ancestors could invent such amazing tales about the gods. Contemporary scientific circles assume that the gods of our past, the gods of myth were creative inventions of fertile minds and probably the product of someone's fanciful imagination. The gods have also been described as representing the forces of the natural world. Some researchers believe that over the millennia we elevated our ancestors to a status where they were worshiped like gods. These flippant justifications do not explain one major point. Why would our ancestors make up and memorize word-for-word such far-fetched and far reaching stories? And then, pass them down from generation to generation? These stories were never portrayed as a work of fiction but instead were described as being true factual accounts of their past.

The same holds true when we speak of all of the marvels recently discovered in the areas of architecture, mathematics and astronomy. Scholars, on the one hand, are quick to point out that we were sophisticated enough to build the pyramids and other megalithic structures found around the world. We could carve, move and construct buildings utilizing huge stones weighing in excess of 100's of thousands of pounds. These stones were then put into position with exacting precision according to precise astronomical alignments. Then, at the same time, these same scholars describe our ancestors as being barely one-step out of living in caves. They also imply, when addressing the stories of the gods that our ancestors were too naive and inept to describe what was in front of their eyes. It does not add up.

Could the assumptions made by mainstream archaeologists and historians be wrong and the bizarre stories told by our ancestors be reliably true tales?

When we first started researching this book we believed an earlier highly advanced human society preceded our own. We are not talking about a group such as the Minoans who had a more advanced civilization than their neighboring Greeks. The society we were searching for had technology, not just a hand full of stone tools. They had an in-depth understanding of building methods and construction, agriculture, astronomy, physics and much more.

Through our research, we have not been able to find any evidence to support pre-existing advanced human civilizations. We were not able to locate large populations of people nor vast city centers. Technology implies that there are individuals who specialize in performing specific tasks. How could they develop the technological advances documented in many of the world's most ancient myths if there were only small pockets of people living on the Earth?

But... What if, just what if, our ancestors, the gods of myth, the gods that were written about, sung about and praised...were not from this world? What if they were not human at all? Yes, we are talking about aliens and alien visitation in our distant past. These beings were technologically superior even to our technological advances today. Through their intervention, (they broke the Prime Directive) we were able to gain access to knowledge and information that is well beyond our current evolutionary state.

As you continue, we ask that you stop and take a hard look at the stories being presented. You will find that if you replace the word god with non-terrestrial, non-human or any word other than human and humanity as we know it, the stories make much more sense. This slight change in perspective provides us with an opportunity to look at our history in a whole new way. From this new viewpoint, we find the pieces of the puzzle finally do fit together and forever changes the picture on top of the box.

People who dismiss the idea of ancient aliens always point to the fact that these ancient visitors left no artifacts: a ray gun, some heavy equipment, anything to support their existence.

Imagine if you will... It is 1,000 years in the future and we have mastered interstellar travel. For whatever reason, we jump into our space ship and travel at warp speed out into the vast sea called space. During our journey, we discover a small backwater planet. The atmospheric and gravitational properties are close to what we require to sustain life but it is different enough that we are unable to build permanent structures on the surface of the planet. A decision is made to stop on this planet anyway and a small band of workers establish a residence deep within the bowels of this unknown world. The mission leaders and the balance of the exploratory party remain on their ship supervising the work being done below.

The amount of supplies and materials we can stow on our imaginary ship is limited. With native materials, we construct primitive but functional equipment, which aids us in the work we are required to do. Being alone in space, we cannot run down to Radio Shack, Home Depot or Wal-Mart to purchase the equipment and tools we need, so we do the best we can with the resources available...

Our imaginary story can continue, but let us instead go back to the original question. Why do we not see evidence of high technology littering archeological sites around the world? Because they had limited "high-tech" resources right from the start. The chance of our finding that one lost screwdriver, left by a small group of aliens hundreds of thousands of years ago, is astronomical.

To accept this as possible, we must first recognize the fact the entire universe is not exactly the same age. Astronomers now know that new stars and their associated planets are born and destroyed. It can take millions and billions of light-years for the announcement of a new star to reach Earth. A planet born billions of years ago could be far older than the Earth. Taking this one-step further, if life began on that planet, its inhabitants could be millions or billions of years older than we are now. If humanity had been civilized for 5,000 years, as we are told, where will we be in a million years? A billion years? Perhaps we will visit a newly emerging planet and be viewed as gods.

There is a fascinating twist to this concept. Many cultures from around the world already believe that a group of people, "the gods" came from the sky.

Before we get into the drama of the gods, we must first turn our attention to the gods themselves. The descriptions of the gods we are about to highlight are general in nature. They are based upon a synopsis of the imagery of the gods found worldwide. We will be taking the most common depictions of the gods and attempt to give you a feel for them, their roles and function. Accounts that are more specific will be provided as we move forward.

Figuring out who is whom in these early cultures can be challenging, especially if you only identify the god or goddess by name. If you look at the attributes associated with each god, especially the most ancient of ones, it is easy to see the similarities between the gods of one culture and the corresponding gods from a vastly different culture and geographical area.

This assessment was made based upon the individual god's iconography. Iconography denotes the depiction of an individual or subject within the context of an image, whether it is a picture, a sculpture or a written description. Symbols have been used in art to identify an individual since the earliest times. Sculptures portraying the demi-god Hercules traditionally show him wearing a lion's skin and holding a club. Moses is customarily shown with small horns, a symbol of authority in the ancient Near East, protruding out of his head. When we see the image of thirteen men sitting around a table, dressed in robes and eating dinner, we quickly associate it with the Christian image of *The Last Supper*.

The changing of the name of a god, from one to another can be seen in the Roman Empire. The Romans took over the Greek pantheon of gods when they conquered the Greeks in 168 BCE. The Greek's Zeus became Rome's Jupiter. Similarly, the Greek god Poseidon became the god Neptune. Who they were, the roles they play in their cosmology, are identical. The same repackaging of gods also happened in Egypt. The god Anubis, during the Old Kingdom in Hermopolis, Egypt, was the guardian and protector of the dead. He was the god of the underworld. During the New Kingdom, Anubis' popularity had diminished. His role as protector of the dead was transferred to Osiris. Anubis was then given a lesser role in the Egyptian pantheon.

Local gods commonly would take on the attributes of the most ancient of gods when the seat of culture shifted from one geographical area to another. Many people are confused in thinking that the new culture is talking about a different god. The old god, instead, was repackaged and a new and improved, more socially acceptable god was created.

As we move forward, try thinking of the gods as a business or corporation. There is the president or board of directors, the Chief Executive Officer (CEO) as well as the various department heads. Moving down the hierarchy, we find managers and supervisors and finally workers. Each of these individuals, regardless of function, high or low, in mythology were "the gods". There were no "people", as we know them today. Only a world filled with gods of one kind or another. What we are attempting to describe in this next section are the movers and shakers of this corporation, the CEO as well as the principal department heads. Their subordinates, the individuals who typically perform specific tasks, unfortunately tend to be caught in the ongoing drama of the gods and this can create confusion when attempting to identify them.

We have all grown up surrounded by images of the gods. I remember, as a child, watching the movie *Jason And The Argonauts* which originally aired in 1963. It tells the story of the mythical hero Jason in his quest for the Golden Fleece. Jason, during his travels, battles with the harpies, a giant bronze statue of Talos, as well as the unforgettable warrior skeletons. He, at the beginning of his quest, found himself transported to Mt. Olympus where he meets Zeus and his wife Hera. I will never forget the images of the gods. Zeus and Hera were enormous in size with respect to Jason. Both had fair complexions and wore long flowing robes. Zeus was depicted with white hair and a full white beard, while Hera wore a crown on her head.

A similar image of God is held in Christianity. God is portrayed as an older Caucasian man, sporting a white beard and wearing white flowing robes. How could we forget Michelangelo's captivating image of the *Creation of Man*, where God's extended finger is touching the index finger of Adam, the first man. It is easy for those born into this tradition to see how we, according to Genesis 1:27, could look like God or he like us.

The gods are often described as tall in stature. Their complexion is depicted as white, yellow or golden in hue. They were reported as having ample golden or red hair and blue eyes. In some traditions, it is said that the faces of the gods gleamed like *"the light of the new risen sun"* or that they had shining bodies. These individuals were in some cultures called "the shining ones".

It is when we move around the globe to the New World that things get interesting. When inhabitants from Mexico to Peru were asked to describe their Creator God, they too describe him as being a bearded Caucasian man in flowing robes. This is fascinating because the indigenous populations of the Americas were not exposed to "the white man" until the arrival of the Spanish in the 1500's. What makes their claim more amazing is that Native Americans do not grow excessive facial hair. A beard among their people is a rare occurrence. This is why the Aztecs, according to legend, welcomed the Spanish conquistadors with open arms. They had a belief that their "god" would one-day return to them. When the Spaniards appeared on their shores, the Aztecs believed them to be gods, and their leader Cortés, to be Quetzalcoatl. Quetzalcoatl was the Creator God of the Aztec people.

The gods, however, are not always described as having human, much less Caucasoid form. The gods, in some representations, are depicted as having wings like those imagined on angels. Hindu and Buddhist traditions depict an array of gods with humanoid or partially humanoid form. For example, Indra, the God of War, is often portrayed with four arms. Brahma, their chief celestial god, is shown with four heads. Their god Vaisravana is represented as a dwarf.

We only have to look at the original Greek pantheon to find more gods depicted in strange ways. The gods Uranus and Gaia had a number of children, which included the Titans, the Hekatonkheires (gods who had 100 arms and 50 heads) and the Cyclopes (gods with only one eye in the center of their heads). Many cultures around the world also describe a race of giant gods.

More than any other descriptions provided regarding the physical appearance of a non-humanoid god form is that of a snake or dragon. There are descriptions of gods who take the form of snakes in every culture around the world. They are described as having the upper body of a man and the lower part of the body resembling a snake. Snake gods include Enki, Queztzalcoatl, Neptune, Ophion and Typhon, Apep, Kanmare, Fu Xi and Nuwa, Jormungand and the Nommo.

It is a mystery to truly know what the gods looked like. The gods are portrayed with the ability to shape-shift. Meaning they could change their outward appearance at will. Quetzalcoatl is described appearing in both human form and in the form of the feathered serpent. In Norse mythology, both Odin and Loki are said to have changed their appearance, where they took female forms, to tempt or spy on one another.

In Greek mythology, Zeus is famous for this shape-shifting skill. He used it to seduce women. It was thought by the ancient Greeks that if Zeus revealed himself in his true form, it would cause instant destruction to mortals. Forms he took included that of a white cow, a white bull, a swan and a satyr. Additionally, Zeus is said to have altered himself into the form of Amphytrion, the son of Alcaeus, the king of Tiryns. He did this in order to seduce Amphytrion's betrothed, Alcmene, the daughter of the king of Mycenae. The demi-god Heracles was the product of this union.

From our investigation, we have uncovered five primary gods, the CEO and his chief department heads. We are also including a review of the Omnipotent Creator God in this section to help show the similarities and differences from a descriptive, iconological point of view. We have chosen to identify these gods using their titles rather than to their names. They include Sky Father, the God of War, the Fertility God, the God of the Underworld and the God of Treasures.

Omnipotent Creator God

The Omnipotent Creator God is the God we described earlier. He is the God who lives external to the world he created. This God, according to the myths that come down to us, existed prior to creation where he supplied the energy for creation to occur. This undetectable God does not have a form, human or otherwise, nor any attributes. This God is believed to be in everything and everywhere and is beyond human comprehension. Cultures such as the Aztec and those of India inform us that this God did not create the Earth and humankind directly, but instead created the gods who facilitated this act. This God in many cultures has been lost or his role has been combined with the attributes of the Sky Father.

This God has been referred to as Ometeotl by the Aztec, Awonawilona by the Zuni's, Vishnu by the Hindus and Waaq by the Oromo people of South Africa. The Native American Indian tribe, the Pawnee relate that this God, Tirawa-atius, could not come near men. Lesser power gods were created who were permitted to mediate between man and this God.

Sky Father

The concept of a "Father God" or "Sky Father" is consistently referred to in the mythos of different cultures. This great god is said to be "formless." Some traditions recognize that no one has ever seen him. It is stated that he came down from the sky during the earliest period of our history. He is often described as having a human face, which is surrounded by the sun, a golden disk, a halo of serpents or the horns of a bull. He is known as the Sky Father, Father Heaven and the Sun Father. In many cultures, his name translates to the words sky, the skies, or heaven. He is believed to reign supreme over all. He is identified as being the great creator as well as judge over the virtues of life on the planet. His wrath is often associated with issues of veneration (or lack thereof) or of mankind not following the laws he provided. Stories of this god often state that he would one-day return to a people or nation.

The Zuni knew this god as Apoyan Tachi, the Inca called him Hunab Ku. The Yoruba tribe of West Africa called him Olorum, the Gaunches of the Canary Islands call him Achamán, An or Anu in Sumeria and Shangdi in China. It is said that he created the rivers, mountains and forests. This god is said to live in the sky but at times descends upon the summits of the mountains where he watches over us.

God of War

A subordinate of the Sky Father is the God of War. The God of War is known under a number of different names including, Sky Spirit, God or Guardian of the Sky, God of War, Chief of all Gods and the Ruler of Heaven. The God of War is responsible for carrying out the judgments of the Sky Father. His wrath has included the annihilation of life on Earth. He presides over the Earth and acts as a mediator between the gods and man. He is often described as being a very angry, vengeful deity who has "issues" when others do not respect his authority.

The God of War is often depicted riding storm clouds and shooting flaming arrows or throwing lightning bolts at humans or the demonic forces. His voice is frequently described as sounding like thunder. The God of War in some cultures represent him holding a pickaxe, hoe, club or hammer. He is associated with birds and the eagle in particular. Some of the names of this god include: Zeus, Enlil, Indra, Hino, Tulpan, Choc, Hurakan and Mamaragan.

Fertility God

The Fertility God is the one who had the closest relationship with mankind. Stories of the Fertility God abound because of his ongoing interaction with humanity. He has many epitaphs and even more names as you travel around the world. He is said to be the god of fertility and plays an indispensible role in the creation of man and the formation of culture. His behavior is like a loving parent. In his paternal role, he taught people how to write, how to use the calendar and to perform healing arts. He is also known as the God of the Watery Deep, where he influences the waters of the Earth. He is often depicted with a three pronged fork like object called a triton in his hand and being able to appear in the form of a serpent, dragon, half-man half-serpent or half-fish. He is traditionally identified as mischievous or as a trickster and has been called Poseidon, Neptune, Queztzalcoatl, Varuna, Enki, Michabo, Baiame, Ngai, Obatala and Itzamna.

God Of The Underworld

Little description survives regarding the God of the Underworld. People did not sing to him, praise him nor venerate him. They did, however, fear him. The God of the Underworld is known worldwide. His realm can be found deep within the Earth or somewhere far below the Earth. The earliest traditions viewed the God of the Underworld not as the god of death, dying and punishment, but rather as the caretaker of his realm where he is associated with the souls of individuals after death. Later traditions describe his abode as a place of punishment for the wicked. He has gone by the names Hades, Lucifer, Yama, Hun-Came and Vucub-Came and Osiris.

God Of Treasures

Even less is known about the God of Treasures. Many traditions do not even acknowledge this god as part of their pantheon. Some texts describe him as being greedy or as a hoarder of his treasures. These treasures included gold, silver and other precious minerals and stones of the world. Some cultures physically describe him as a dwarf. In other cultures he is some kind of horned, pointy toothed or hairy monster. In yet others he is described as a giant. He is said to live underground in caves, under mountains or in the woods. He and those under his command are identified as master builders, architects, and the designers of the advanced technology used by the gods. Names associated with this god include Hephaestus and Vishvakarman.

Sometimes the role of a specific god is combined with, and attributed to, a different god. For example, in the Judeo-Christian tradition the one and only god takes on the characteristics of the Creator God, the Sky Father, the God of War and some of the attributes of the Fertility God. He and his work is not supported by other gods, but instead by angels, which are not classified as gods. The qualities connected to the God of the Underworld as well as some of the features of the Fertility God have been combined into the role of God's arch-nemesis, the fallen angel Lucifer, better known as the Devil.

The Greek pantheon of gods report a division of three god-heads, Zeus, the Sky Father/God of War, Neptune, the Fertility God and Hades, the God of the Underworld. The role of master builders, architects and designers are attached to monstrous members of the Titan race of gods who seem to not have any official standing. This same convention of combining gods is seen, depending on the culture, worldwide. Why this has happened is a mystery.

Even with all of the confusion surrounding the naming of the gods, historians cannot explain how cultures such as the Sumerians, Indians (of India), Greeks, Norse, Native Americans as well as the Aborigines of Australia all reference gods with similar attributes in parallel ways. Why is the God of War always associated with thunder and lightning? Why is the Fertility God always connected with water? If individuals in these remote cultures were only fabricating these stories, the potential variety of characteristics that could be associated with any of these gods would be astronomical. Interestingly, that is not what we find. We find a finite number of attributes associated with the gods, especially the gods of the early pantheon. These characteristics are shared among cultures worldwide. The uncanny parallel in descriptors associated with these gods only makes sense if each of the diverse cultures were talking about a single god or group of gods!

Who Art In Heaven

The current Christian concept of heaven is of a place where God dwells. It is also the home to God's messengers, the angels. It is associated with eternal life. It is where people, who have lived virtuous lives, go and live for time without end in peace, prosperity and happiness in a virtual paradise. Heaven is not on or off the Earth. It is recognized as being located somewhere in the sky, but exactly where? Is it possible that heaven is not just a vague place "up there"? Could it be an actual destination like San Francisco, Tibet or Tahiti?

In the story of Moses and the Exodus from Egypt, God for a short time, could be found on the top of Mount Sinai. God appearing on a mountain is not an exclusive event, which can only be found in the Bible. Mountains are described as the home of the gods worldwide. Zeus was said to live on the top of Mount Olympus. The Lord Brahma lived on Mount Meru. The supreme ruler of the gods in China, the Jade Emperor, Yu Hang, could be found on the summit of one of the K'un-lun mountain peaks. The Japanese gods resided on Mt. Fuji. The mountain top city of Machu Picchu, in Peru, was originally called Yllampu. This word spoken by the Inca translates as the "City of the Gods."

The gods, according to legend, only came down to the surface of the Earth when needed. They did not live on Earth all the time. It appears as if they came down to the Earth to take care of some administrative duty associated with running the planet. When they were here, they would take up temporary residence on the tops of the mountains and then leave when their work was completed.

The word heaven is said to have originally signified the sky or firmament above. Some cultures view heaven as a floating island somewhere out in space. In China, the pictogram (a form of writing using representational, pictorial drawings as opposed to letters) for the word sky or heaven is "tian". The word tian is one of the oldest Chinese terms for the cosmos. The earliest inscription for the word tian (see figure 1) is represented by what appears to be a humanoid form with outstretched arms, denoting "great" or "large". The cranium of this great person is also emphasized. Could the original meaning of the word tian actually signify the deities who lived in the heavens rather than the concept of the sky or heavens above?

Figure 1 - Chinese Oracle script for *tian* 天 "heaven"

Olympus, according to Greek mythology is the celestial abode of the Sky God Zeus. Olympus was located on or above Mount Olympus. Built by the Cyclopes, and designed by Hephaestus, it was positioned in a place believed by the Greeks to be unreachable by birds. It was said to extend out beyond the clouds and far into the ether. It is described as having an ethereal atmosphere that was glistening to the eyes. The environment was said to have a calming influence over the hearts and minds of its inhabitants. It was well understood that the inhabitants of Olympus did not age, thus if a mere mortal reached the halls of Olympus they would now be immortal, the true sign of being a god.

Zeus' palace is depicted as constructed with burnished gold, chased silver and gleaming ivory. Zeus' enormous throne was made of polished black marble with a golden eagle perched on its right arm. Hera, his wife, sat on a throne of ivory. A full moon hung above it. The back of her throne was decorated with golden cuckoos and willow leaves. Olympus was not only Zeus' home but was the home to many of the gods and demi-gods. Their homes, depending on their rank, were less commanding in size and were constructed of silver, ebony, ivory and brass.

Not all of the gods lived in the heavens. Heaven was reserved for the Sky God. The other gods are said to live in and around mountains, the underworld or beneath its waters. None of the accounts researched describe a god who lived on the surface of the Earth. In Greek mythology, Poseidon had a residence on Olympus, which he visited when he would meet with the counsel of gods. His beloved palace, however, was located at the bottom of the sea. His palace was filled with vast halls in which thousands of his followers could assemble. It was filled with fountains and plants and was topped by a glistening dome. The walkways are even said to have been covered with sparkling sand mixed with amber, pearls and other precious jewels. Beautiful plants, tall grasses and groves of coralline surrounded his palace. His abode, even though it was located deep underwater, did not lack for light. The glow-worms of the deep sea illuminated it.

Likewise, the Greek god Hades' home was not found in the sky but in the underworld. His subterranean realm is described as a place where the sunlight never shines. The underworld is the realm of the dead. It is where human souls go to rest in peace. It was also the location of "Tartarus" where the Titans, the early Greek gods were imprisoned. Tartarus, as time moved on, was described as a place where people who had committed the worst crimes were sent. Entry and exit into the underworld was difficult. A number of creatures, such as the three-headed hound Cerberus, guarded it. Once inside, one could gain access to the underworld by crossing the river Styx. By paying the ferryman a small fee, one could get safely to the other side.

The Greeks are not the only cultures offering detailed descriptions of the realms of the gods. The dwelling place of the gods can also be found in the second book of the *Mahabharata*. The *Mahabharata* is an ancient Indian Sanskrit epic. In a conversation between Yudhishthira, the son of Pandu and Narada the divine sage, Narada describes the "*sabhas*", the assembly rooms of Yama, Varuna, Sakra (Indra), Vaisravana (Kubera) and Aditya. Narada tells Yudhishthira that each of these assembly rooms were enormous in size and were capable of housing hundreds of thousands of people. The smallest of them, the *sabha* of Vaisravana, was said to be 100 *yojanas* in length by 70 *yojanas* in breadth. A *yojanas* is the distance an ox cart can travel in one day. While the exact number is contested, the distance of a *yohonas* is estimated at somewhere between five to twelve miles in length. If these numbers are correct and a *yojanas* is five miles in length then the *sabha* of Vaisravana was 500 miles in length by 350 miles in width.

Each of the *sabhas* according to Narada was capable of going anywhere at the will of its owner. Even though they could move and travel around the skies, they were associated with a specific cardinal point on the Earth: Vaisvarana with the North; Yama with the South, Sakra with the East and Varuna with West. Vishvakarman, the divine carpenter and master builder of the gods built the *sabhas*. Vishvakarman also fashioned the weapons of the gods and their celestial chariots.

Sakra, the Lord of the Heavens, had assembly rooms described as being filled with luster and possessing the splendor of the sun. Sakra, and his wife, Sachi, are seen sitting on magnificent thrones. Sakra's assembly rooms, like Zeus', are said to dispel the weakness of age, grief, fatigue and fear. The halls are filled with the other great gods as well as some of the lesser ones. People of wisdom, all of whom possess pure souls whose sins "*have been completely washed off*", also live there. Individuals of great ascetic merit also inhabit it as well as those whose speech is always truthful. Each of these individuals waits upon and worships Sakra, "*the illustrious chief of the immortals, that mighty repressor of all foes.*" Residence in the assembly rooms was not permanent. The gods were free to come and go by means of their celestial chariots.

Bright as burnished gold is how Yama's *sabha* is described. Yama is the God of Death, a position similar to Hades, the Greek god of the underworld. His *sabha* is said to possess the spender of the sun and contain everything one may desire. Old age, weakness, hunger and thirst do not exist in his abode. In this *sabha* there is hot and cold water and is filled with fruit trees. Here, royal sages and virtuous persons of great sanctity and purity take up residence. It is home to men of great wisdom, knowledge and achievements. The occupants of this *sabha* spend all of their time waiting upon and worshiping Yama, the God of Justice.

Varuna, the Lord of Waters, *sabha* is said to be unparalleled in splendor. His *sabha* finds its home within the watery depths. Its walls are pure white and are surrounded by many fruit bearing trees made of gems and jewels. Birds fill the home of Varuna. Varuna is waited upon by a multitude of celestial beings as well as the nagas, a class of entities or deities that take the form of great snakes. Men of great bravery, who excel in, or faithfully fulfill their vows, also surround him. Aquatic animals of all kind worship Varuna in his *sabha*.

The fourth *sabha* is Vaisravana's. Vaisravana (Kubera) is the Lord of Wealth and the natural treasures hidden in the Earth. His abode is described as "*possessing the splendor of the peaks of Kailasa, that mansion eclipses by its own the brilliance of the moon himself*". Its chambers are depicted as constructed of pure gold, spotted with countless gems. Its halls are filled with forests of tall mandaras and fragrant plants of all kinds. The *Mahabharata* continues telling us that he is surrounded by "*multitudes of spirits in the hundreds and thousands, some of dwarfish stature, some of fierce visage, some hunch-backed, some of blood-red eyes, some of frightful yells, some feeding upon fat and flesh, and some terrible to behold, but all armed with various weapons*". Each of these individuals wait upon and worship Vaisravana.

The fifth and final *sabha* belongs to the exalted deity Aditya. According to Narada, Aditya, during the Krita Yuga, came down from heaven and wandered the Earth in human form. Aditya's *sabha* is said to be immeasurable, immaterial and indescribable. It had the ability to change its shape and form thus making a description of it virtually impossible. This *sabha* was stationed in heaven, forever eternal and surpassing in splendor both the sun and the moon. It is the home of the elemental and primal causes of the universe, the vital principles and the Vedas.

The belief in great houses created by the gods is supported in Sumerian mythology. William Hallo (Hallo, 1971) indicates that there were five great antediluvian cities in Sumer. They were known for their "high location" and were referred to as "lofty cities." These cities were highly regarded for their exalted status. According to Hallo, "*In mythological terms, however, it was the cosmic "eternal city" ([UR]U sa-a-tú), [that was] built by Heaven and Earth themselves.*"

From the tale of *Gilgamesh and Aga* we learn of Inanna's House of Heaven, E-ana. Inanna is the Sumerian goddess of sexual love, fertility, and warfare. She is also known as the Lady of the Sky.

The great gods created the structure of Unug, the handiwork of the gods, and of E-ana, the house lowered down from heaven. You watch over its great rampart, a cloudbank resting on the earth, the majestic residence which An established... - Gilgamesh and Aga

We find several descriptions of the dwelling place of the Sumerian Fertility God Enki whose home was located in the watery deep. His domain is called *E-en-gur-a*, which is translated as "the house of the subterranean waters".

The lord established a shrine, a holy shrine, whose interior is elaborately constructed. He established a shrine in the sea, a holy shrine, whose interior is elaborately constructed. The shrine, whose interior is a tangled thread, is beyond understanding. The shrine's emplacement is situated by the constellation the Field, the holy upper shrine's emplacement

66

faces towards the Chariot constellation. Its terrifying sea is a rising wave, its splendour is fearsome. The Anuna gods dare not approach it. - Enki And The World Order

> *The lord of the abyss, the king Enki,*
> *Enki, the lord who decrees the fates,*
> *Built his house of silver and lapis lazuli;*
> *Its silver and lapis lazuli, like sparkling light,*
> *The father fashioned fittingly in the abyss.*
> *The (creatures of) bright countenance and wise, coming forth from the abyss,*
> *Stood all about the lord Nudimmud;*
> *The pure house be built, he adorned it with lapis lazuli,*
> *He ornamented it greatly with gold.*
> - Enki And Eridu: The Journey Of The Water God To Nippur

The concept of different realms of the gods crosses the globe where it is found in Amerindian cosmology in the myths of the Aztecs, the Mayas of Yucatan and the Kiches and Cakchiquels of Guatemala. The *Annals of the Cakchiquels* and the *Memorial de Solola* report on the dwelling of Quetzalcoatl and the land of his origin. These texts recount an ancient Cakchiquel legend, which describes something called the Tulan (Tollan or Tonatlan), "the place of the sun". Quetzalcoatl's Tulan is described as a land filled with crops of maize that grew to the length of a man's arm. These crops are reported never to fail. Cotton could be grown here not only in white but in all colors under the rainbow. It was filled with beautiful birds. Melodious songs filled the air. The houses were built of silver and precious stones. Like the realms in Sumeria, Greece and India, it is from this domain that the servants of Quetzalcoatl could fly to any part of the world with infinite speed.

According to their legends, there is not only one Tulan, the home of Quetzalcoatl but a total of four.

Where the sun rises, there is one Tulan ; another is in the underworld; yet another where the sun sets ; and there is

67

still another, and there dwells the God. Thus, O my children, there are four Tulans, as the ancient men have told us. - Annals of the Cakchiquels

> *... Q'aq'awitz and Saqtekaw said:*
> *"It was four (locations),*
> *where people came from Tulan:*
> *in the east is one Tulan;*
> *another one there in Xib'alb'ay;*
> *another one there in the west,*
> *the one where we come from*
> *is in the west;*
> *another one there in K'ab'owil.*
> - Memorial de Sololá - Adrián Recinos

From the Navaho Creation Myth, the *Hahdenigai-Hunai,* we learn that the blue-eyed, yellow-haired great god Begochiddy was one of the six gods who first inhabited the dark Earth. He went on to build five "colored mountains" called Tsilth-náh-n'deeldói on the Earth. The word Tsilth-náh-n'deeldói when translated means colored mountains which appear and disappear. The mountains were constructed with one in each of the four directions, North, South, East and West. The final mountain was built in the center of the world.

If you found what was just described hard to believe, the tales that come out of Norse mythology will seem as if they came from out of this world - literally. Viking culture extended from Iceland, through the Netherlands into Germany and the Scandinavian countries. Like many oral traditions, Norse mythology is often discounted because of its late arrival into the cosmological world. This is attributed to the fact that their tales were not written down until around the 13th Century. It is also believed that many of their stories were corrupted by the already well established Christian faith. As you read excerpts from the poetic tales that come from this cultural group you quickly discover that the perceived connection of their mythology to Christianity is anything but a fallacy.

From the Nordic people we find a belief in the existence of something called a world tree. It is called Yggdrasil in the books of prose, which document Norse lore. These books are called the *Eddas*. The world tree is the home of nine separate planets or realms each inhabited by a different race of beings. These realms include:

- Asgard – The world of the Aesir or Sky Gods
- Vanaheim – The world of the Vanir the Fertility Gods
- Ljossalfheim - The world of the Light Elves
- Midgard – The middle world or middle earth, the home of humans
- Muspellsheim – The world of the fire giants
- Svartalfheim – The world of the Black Elves or Dwarves
- Jotunheim – The world of the Rock and Ice Giants
- Helheim – Abode of the Dead
- Nifelheim – Realm of Ice

Travel between Asgard and the Earth, according to the *Prose Edda Story of Gylfaginning*, was by means of a bridge called Bifröst. Bifröst was built by the gods and when in use appeared as a rainbow in the sky. Andy Orchard (Orchard, 1997) suggests that Bifrost may mean "shimmering path". Based upon the etymology of the word, the verb *bifa,* means "to shimmer" or "to shake" which may indicate the lustrous sheen of the bridge. A second "rainbow bridge" was required if one wanted to travel to the underworld and reach the house of Hel, Helheim.

There is worldwide support for the incredible tales that come to us from the Vikings. The rainbow, in many early cultures, was seen as a pathway between the Earth and the heavenly realms as well as the other Earthly realms. In Japan, it was called the "Floating Bridge of Heaven". North American Indian tribes describe it as the "Pathway of Souls". The "Path to the Upper world" is how it is described in Hawaii and Polynesia. Virtuous, honorable and righteous individuals, in some cultures, are said to travel via the rainbow to the afterlife or go to the world of the gods. Irish folklore tells us that there is a leprechaun's pot of gold at the end of the rainbow.

What were our ancestors trying to describe? Could they be talking about something like a transporter beam, a wormhole or other means of transportation from the Earth to the other godly realms?

The concept of a "World Tree" or "Tree of Life" is also found worldwide. The World Tree, according to many ancient traditions, supports or holds up the cosmos while providing a link between heaven, Earth and the underworld. It is depicted with its branches reaching up into the sky and its roots buried deep within the Earth.

The World Tree, for example, was an important part of Mayan cosmology where it represents the four cardinal points as well as the four-fold nature of the universe. It is home to the Four Wind Gods (Bacabab) who support the four corners of the Earth. Called "ua-hom-che", the term is translated as "Tree of Bread" or the "High Tree of Life". In Mayan art, the Tree of Life is represented with its roots extending deeply into the earth and birds in its branches. It is sometimes shown with the quetzal bird resting on the top of its branches and a serpent lying around its base. Carvings of the Tree of Life in China are depicted with a representation of a phoenix as well as a dragon within its branches and base. Around the world in the savannah region of Africa the baobab tree is referred to as the Tree of Life. The Tree of Life, in Jewish Mysticism is composed of 10 worlds (Sephirot) with each world representing an emanation of God.

Other cultures include the concept of other worlds, planets or realms. The Chinese Yellow Emperor, Huang Di's palace extended nine stories into the sky as well as nine stories into the Earth. One could gain access to both the underworld as well as the realms of the gods by means of his palace. The Aztecs and Toltecs believed that the heavens were constructed of thirteen separate levels. This tradition is also supported in India where we learn:

70

Beyond the sun there are other planetary systems where persons who are elevated by great austerities and penances are situated. The entire material universe is called Devidhama, and above it there is Sivadhama, where Lord Siva and his wife Parvati eternally reside. Above that planetary system is the spiritual sky where innumerable spiritual planets, known as Vaikunthas, are situated. Above these Vaikuntha planets there is Krishna's planet known as Goloka Vrindavana. - The Teachings Of Lord Caitanya

Lowest of all is located Devi-dhama, next above it is Mahesa-dama; above Mahesa-dhama is placed Hari-dhama and above them all is located Krishna's own realm named Goloka. - Brahma-Samhita

Christianity also has a long-standing tradition of "beings" that live in other realms. These beings are called angels. Angels are separated into nine distinct orders and live in nine separate realms. They are identified from highest to lowest as the Seraphim, the Cherubim, the Thrones, the Dominions, the Virtues, the Powers, the Principalities, the Archangels and finally the Angels. The angels include well-known figures such as Michael, Gabriel, Raphael, and of course the fallen angel, Lucifer.

Spiritual traditions speculate that the worlds or realms identified in mythology represent planes of spiritual existence rather than real tangible places. They believe that these planes incorporate concepts such as material creation, consciousness, the ego, the intellect and our spiritual connection with God. They are not seen as being physical in nature, instead they represent aspects of our spiritual development and ourselves.

If the worlds being described by these cultures were only aspects of our higher selves then why would we need to invent an omnipotent god to run the show? In turn, if the gods only exist on non-material or spiritual planes, the "beings", people or races that inhabit these worlds would be non-corporeal in nature. It does seem clear from accounts provided by some of the most primitive cultures around the world that they could tell the difference between a person and a non-corporeal being like a ghost. Their gods are never referred to as taking on an ethereal, spiritual or ghostlike form.

The Gods & Their Toys

When we think of God, we often imagine a being who is able to manifest at will whatever he desires. Like a magician, with one wave of his hand, a wink of his eye or the wiggle of his nose, it comes into existence. This is not what we found when we investigated the gods of our past. It was hard not to notice, when we read these ancient stories, the incredible technology the gods possessed. It is also difficult to overlook their complete and utter reliance on technology in their daily lives. The amazing devices the gods utilized were not made manifest by the Creator God. Myth tells us that they, as well as their homes, were built by master builders: the giants, dwarfs and monsters that live within the mountain and are associated with the God of Treasures.

The gods, using this technology, are purported to have had the ability to transport themselves over incredible distances. Travel was not based upon the nod of a god's head. Instead, it is by means of a miraculous vehicle. Stories of these incredible vehicles are found worldwide. They are described as golden, shining or magic flying chariots. These craft flew through the air and sky and were often recounted as being drawn by horses or some other celestial beast. They are said to be able to travel over land or sea and appeared to have no limitation in time or space. The gods used these vehicles to navigate the Earth as well as to travel back and forth to the heavens. One of these chariots is depicted in the biblical story of Elijah.

And it came about that as they were walking along, speaking as they walked, why, look! a fiery war chariot and fiery horses, and they proceeded to make a separation between them both; and Elijah went ascending in the windstorm to the heavens. All the while Elisha was seeing it, and he was crying out: "My father, my father, the war chariot of Israel and his horsemen!" And he did not see him anymore. – 2 Kings 2:11 - 12

Others describe the arrival and departure of the gods as traveling in flying fireballs. Some are reported as mounting a seat on a cloud and flying off into the heavens. In other cultures the gods are said to descend and ascend to the Earth in a fog or an iridescent cloud. Also mentioned as methods of transportation are a variety of birds, with the eagle being the most common, serpents as well as dragons.

Movement of these craft was anything but stealthy. They are accompanied by thunder, lightning, rain and blackened skies. The Sanskrit epic, the *Ramayana*, informs us that these atmospheric anomalies often alerted the gods of the arrival of a divine guest.

The Gods themselves from every sphere,
Incomparably bright,
Borne in their golden cars drew near
To see the wondrous sight.
The cloudless sky was all aflame
With the light of a hundred suns
Where'er the shining chariots came
That bore those holy ones.
So flashed the air with crested snakes
And fish of every hue
As when the lightning's glory breaks
Through fields of summer blue.
And white foam-clouds and silver spray
Were wildly tossed on high,

Like swans that urge their homeward way
Across the autumn sky.
- The Ramayana

The Bible provides us with a second detailed description of the arrival of one of these godly craft. It had been three months since Moses lead the Israelites out of Egypt and into the desert. When they arrived at Mount Sinai, God, via Moses, commanded the people to obey his (God's) rules and commands. If they did, they would become "a kingdom of priests and a holy nation". God wanted to make sure his "chosen people" were doing what he requested. He decided to have a one-on-one with his people it seems. He believed that if the people could hear his words directly they would be able to put their faith in him (God) and Moses. God let Moses know that the meeting was scheduled to take place in three days. This is the biblical account of God's visit to the people of Israel.

And on the third day when it became morning it came about that thunders and lightnings began occurring, and a heavy cloud upon the mountain and a very loud sound of a horn, so that all the people who were in the camp began to tremble. Moses now brought the people out of the camp to meet the [true] God, and they went taking their stand at the base of the mountain. And Mount Sinai smoked all over, due to the fact that Jehovah came down upon it in fire; and its smoke kept ascending like the smoke of a kiln, and the whole mountain was trembling very much. When the sound of the horn became continually louder and louder, Moses began to speak, and the [true] God began to answer him with a voice. – Exodus 19:16 - 19

Now all the people were seeing the thunders and the lightning flashes and the sound of the horn and the mountain smoking. When the people got to see it, then they quivered and stood at a distance. And they began to say to

Moses: "You speak with us, and let us listen; but let not God speak with us for fear we may die." So Moses said to the people: "Do not be afraid, because for the sake of putting YOU to the test the [true] God has come, and in order that the fear of him may continue before YOUR faces that YOU may not sin." And the people kept standing at a distance, but Moses went near to the dark cloud mass where the [true] God was. – Exodus 20:18 - 21

Grand celestial palaces and flying chariots were not the only pieces of advanced technology the gods had at their disposal. They also had magnificent but lethal weapons. The Archangel Michael is associated with his sword of truth. Zeus, Jupiter and Enlil are known for throwing lightning and thunder bolts at their enemies with devastating effect. The trident, a three-pronged spear wielded by Poseidon, Neptune, Enki, Shiva and Aegir is celebrated for its ability to shake up the Earth, where it causes earthquakes, tidal waves and tsunamis.

The Norse god Thor is traditionally pictured carrying his mighty hammer called Mjölnir. Mjölnir, in some texts, is described as an ax, club or a hammer. It was recognized, regardless of its appearance, as a weapon, which could level mountains. The *Prose Edda* informs us that Thor, with Mjölnir in hand, could aim it at something and strike it unfailingly. If, as legend tells, he threw his hammer, in addition to never missing its target, it would always find its way back to his hand.

Interestingly, in Australia, the two Wati Kutjara brothers wielded the magical boomerang, Wo-mur-rang or club. Boomerangs are known for their ability, once thrown, to return to the thrower. They used it to castrate their father Kidili. Half way around the world, we find in Greek mythology that a sickle (a weapon that looks surprisingly similar to a boomerang) was used by the god Cronus to castrate his father Uranus. We also find the sickle described in Sumerian lore. In the *Hymn To Enlil-Bani*, the sickle was Enlil's weapon without rival.

Other weapons of myth include Chun-T'i's luminous bow, No-cha's Heaven -and-Earth bracelet, Innana's a-an-kar weapon and Manco Capac's golden wand. The legend of *Hua-hu Tiao Devours Yang Chien* describes a magical spike carried by Huang T'ien Hua.

The Chin-kang, deprived of their magical weapons, began to lose heart. To complete their discomfiture, Huang T'ien Hua brought to the attack a matchless magical weapon. This was a spike 7 1/2 inches long, enclosed in a silk sheath, and called 'Heart-piercer.' It projected so strong a ray of light that eyes were blinded by it. Huang T'ien Hua, hard pressed by Mo-li Ch'ing, drew the mysterious spike from its sheath, and hurled it at his adversary. It entered his neck, and with a deep groan the giant fell dead. - Myths & Legends of China – E. T. C. Werner

Could the magical weapon carried by Huang T'ien Hua be the same as the one wielded by the Greek god Zeus? The devastating effects of this same weapon can be found in the writings of Hesoid. It tells of the battle between Zeus and Typhoeus (Typhon), the deadliest monster in Greek mythology.

Typhoeus was hurled down, a maimed wreck, so that the huge earth groaned. And flame shot forth from the thunder-stricken lord in the dim rugged glens of the mount, when he was smitten. A great part of huge earth was scorched by the terrible vapour and melted as tin melts when heated by men's art in channelled crucibles; or as iron, which is hardest of all things, is softened by glowing fire in mountain glens and melts in the divine earth through the strength of Hephaistos. Even so, then, the earth melted in the glow of the blazing fire [i.e. to form volcanoes]. And in the bitterness of his anger Zeus cast him into wide Tartaros... - Theogony of Hesiod

77

Another example of the destructive capability of these weapons can be found in the Sumerian text *The Exploits Of Ninurta*, which tells of Ninurta's battle with the monster Asag. In this clash, Ninurta uses his mace called Car-ur to battle his foe.

The mace snarled at the Mountains, the club began to devour all the enemy. He fitted the evil wind and the sirocco on a pole (?), he placed the quiver on its hook (?). An enormous hurricane, irresistible, went before the Hero, stirred up the dust, caused the dust to settle, leveled high and low, filled the holes. It caused a rain of coals and flaming fires; the fire consumed men. It overturned tall trees by their trunks, reducing the forests to heaps... The Exploits of Ninurta

Pretty amazing stuff!

Before we move on, let us bring this concept full circle and back into a present cultural context. Are our myths informing us that we are actually part of some kind of a federation of planets? Did ships the size of the triangular Star Destroyers, the signature vessel of the Imperial fleet seen in the Star Wars saga, visit the Earth?

It is easy for us in this modern age to envision this possibility. We have been provided with images of extraterrestrial beings such as Vulcans, Romulans, Klingons and Andorians. We have, in the world of science fiction, traveled to galaxies far, far away on starships and battle cruisers. These visions are supported by the measure of the technology we currently possess yet at the same time we still see them as make believe and fantasy. On the flip side, there is a level of conviction that one day we will develop the technology to explore the stars and travel to the far reaches of space.

The key question remains unchanged. How did our ancestors create such colorful stories? It is easy to believe that we borrowed these ancient tales from our ancestors and transformed them into contemporary settings. It is much harder to believe that our forefathers came up with these stories on their own.

It is human nature to take something that is known and transform it into something else. The gods and the level of technology they possessed are far beyond anything remotely associated with our predecessor's worldview - that is, unless it was part of their world. As they say, truth is stranger than fiction - so perhaps the stories they are telling are true.

The Original
Shock & Awe

Cycles Of Time

It is difficult to trace solid evidence back to the earliest recorded times. We only retain dim memories of our most distant past. The details we do know are only alluded to in myths. The majority of cultures produce a broad brush regarding the earliest of times. It is, however, from this point that we will begin putting together the pieces of our past. We do find something remarkable when we canvas these long forgotten stories from cultures around the world. While the names of the gods are changed and minor details are altered, repackaged and sometimes eliminated, the basis of our story remains congruent. In the texts that follow, we will be providing myths that tell of our unfolding history. The tales they tell are incredible. What is presented is not exclusive, but a sampling of stories told by our ancestors from around the world.

Details from our myths also helped us to arrive at the timeline we are about to share. All of the stories we obtained are thinly veiled in cultural influences. This makes them appear to be different on the surface. By lining up particulars such as the usurping of power from one generation to the next, the creation and formation of the Earth, and the wars between the gods, it becomes evident that the stories being told are the same. These parallel facts provide milestones on which we aligned our chronology into a coherent story line.

Some of the legends we discovered begin with the arrival of the gods and follow a clear and concise timeline of the great many events which have transpired throughout time. Others begin with creation then jump forward in time, returning to the story line later in its narrative. There are also cultures that stand mute regarding the details of their history. When they do speak, the consistency of their chronicles from the most archaic tales and primitive cultures to the relatively modern ones is remarkable.

We will be using concepts like the world being submerged under water as a marker in time. When we lined up the stories of our world being submerged beneath water, the accounts that both precede it and follow it miraculously matched. These parallels were not only found regionally but in myths from around the globe. Statistically speaking, the chances of cultures from around the world conjuring up the same stories out of thin air are enormous. The only thing that makes sense is if they were all telling the same story. As we move forward in this text, we will also be looking at the historical record and will be comparing it to the stories that are relayed to us through mythology.

According to the accepted current worldview, the Sumerians in Mesopotamia around 4500 BCE began civilization on the Earth. Mesopotamia was located in the area of the Tigris and Euphrates rivers, which corresponds roughly to modern-day Iraq. Mesopotamia is considered to be the cradle of civilization and home to the forefathers to modern culture. It was the Sumerians, for example, who developed the first form of writing and prescribed the first set of laws. They are known for agricultural and architectural achievements as well as their advanced understanding of astronomy and mathematics. The level of civilization displayed by the Sumerians, if you are to believe the musings of some contemporary historians, appeared out of nowhere and was fully operational and functional from its inception.

Primitive cultures worldwide acknowledge a history that is far older than is presently accepted. These groups recognize that the world has experienced a number of cycles or epochs of time that extend farther into our distant past. Hindu tradition states that this world has existed through a number of extended time periods called yugas. Cultures from the Americas including the Aztecs, Mayans, Hopi and Incas also view our history in cycles of time. The Aztec refer to them as the "Ages of the World" or "Suns".

Similarly, Greeks such as Hesiod recount a series of ages that have transpired throughout time. The majority of the cultures that provide insights into these ancient times unfortunately do not provide dates or timeframes. The dates that are furnished, after a careful examination, do not hold up to scrutiny. They do though provide a chronology of sorts of how and when our history unfolded.

The Hindu Puranas describe time as a number of cycles within cycles. The history of the world, according to these ancient texts, is broken into the days, nights, years and lifetime of the god Brahma. His emergence established the "beginning of time". The smallest of these cycles is called a maha yuga. One maha yuga, according to these texts lasts for 4,320,000 human years.

Each yuga is subsequently subdivided into four epochs whose lengths follow a ratio of 4:3:2:1 (4, 3, 2, and 1 times an interval of 432,000 years). The yugas include the Satya Yuga, the Treta Yuga, the Dwapar Yuga and the Kali Yuga. The first yuga, the Satya Yuga, lasted for 1,728,000 years, the Treta Yuga, for 1,296,000 years, and the Dwapar for 864,000 years. It is believed that we are now in the Kali Yuga, which started on the day Krishna, the eighth incarnation of Hindu god Vishnu, died in 3102 BC. The Kali Yuga is to last for 432,000.

1,728,000	–	432,000	=	1,296,000
1,296,000	–	432,000	=	864,000
864,000	–	432,000	=	432,000
432,000	–	432,000	=	0
4,320,000	Total number of years in 1 Yuga Cycle			

Table 2: Breakdown of the Maha Yuga

One day or *kalpa* in the life of Brahma requires 1,000 maha yuga's to fill. Thus a day in the life of Brahma lasts for 4,320,000,000 (4.32 billion) human-years. It takes two *kalpas* or 8.64 billion human years to account for one full day and night of Brahma. A year of Brahma is composed of 360 day/night cycles of Brahma, or 720 *kalpas*, or 3.11 trillion human years.

The lifespan of Brahma is 100 Brahma years, or 72,000 *kalpas*, or 311.04 trillion human years

Figure 2: The Aztec Calendar, or The Stone of the Five Eras

The Mayans, Aztecs and other Native American cultures also recorded time through a series of epoch periods. Mayan legend and textual evidence recounts "five suns" or five great cycles of time in which the Earth was destroyed and then recreated. It is believed that these five suns or five eras of the world have been memorialized on the Sun Stone, or The Stone of the Five Eras.

More popularly known as the "Aztec Calendar", this 25-ton megalithic stone sculpture was discovered in Zócalo, Mexico City in 1790

Like many of the examples we have discussed so far, there is much speculation regarding the length of each "sun" in Mayan cosmology. Each sun, according to some researchers, has a duration of 9,360,000 days, or 25,625 years. This timing corresponds to a concept that is known as the "precession of the equinoxes". Others propose the length of time described by our Central American ancestors is 25,625 years in total. This is then broken down into the five ages of 5,125 years. It is held that our current age, the fifth sun, began in 3113 BCE and would conclude on December 21, 2012. Regardless of which hypothesis you believe, it is generally accepted that we are currently in the fifth and final Sun.

There is often confusion when trying to differentiate between the concept of worlds or ages. Some cultures provide us with information regarding five separate ages, while others only four. We will be tracking time and unfolding the saga of the gods using Five Ages or Five Worlds as markers in time. We will also look to explain the discrepancies between these two systems of time keeping and attempt to provide a cogent theory regarding why this occurred.

Many people now accept as a fact that the creation of the world did not happen in 4004 BCE as proposed by James Ussher in 1650 CE. It is commonly acknowledged that the formation of our galaxy occurred around 4.5 billion years ago, with the development of life on the Earth commencing not long after.

Starting with the beginning of time on Earth we were left with many unanswered questions. They include when did the gods walk the Earth? What were they doing here? When was man created and why? We do not have all of the answers, but we would like to conjecture as to when these things might have occurred. The theory we are about to propose is based upon clues provided in the mythological record. When our mythological history is compared to what we know from the historical and archeological record, what we find is that intelligent life has been on, under and around our planet for far longer than is currently believed.

Emergence

The earliest and most universally recorded recollection of our history tells us in the beginning, nothing existed. Our world, our universe was a giant watery abyss, a sea of nothingness, chaos. Few details survive regarding the next step in our creation. We learned from the Hindu tradition that Manu-Vishnu, by means of a lotus that sprouted from his navel, a cosmic egg manifested, which ultimately became our universe. In the Egyptian Creation Myth, we are told that out of Nun, the great waters, a great shining egg emerged. Other Egyptian creation myths inform us that a celestial birth or ibis laid the egg. The Greeks attribute the creation of the cosmic egg, a "golden egg", to a bird with big black wings.

After a long period of inertia, eons as some of the stories say, the egg cracked open and the first of the primordial gods, the parents of creation came forward. The top of the egg is traditionally associated with the Sky Father, the bottom, the Earth Mother. The Maori inform us that Sky Father and Earth Mother were held in a tight embrace and were forced apart by their children who lived in the darkness between them. According to Sumerian legends, heaven and earth were once inseparable until heaven and earth were cleaved into two parts.

Some traditions in India tell us that everything existed in the cosmic egg, including the gods, the demons, humans, the sun, the moon, the stars, the planets and the wind. A parallel myth can be found in the tradition of the Seminole and Apache Indians. According to the Seminoles, God created the Earth and all of the animals. He then put them into a large shell and waited for the

Earth to become ready. Time passed and God placed the shell onto the Earth. More time passed until the shell cracked open thus allowing all of the animals out to inhabit the Earth.

A number of dual gods emerge from the union of the Sky Father and the Earth Mother. These primordial gods are often characterized by mainstream cosmologists as being associated with the natural world and the forces of nature such as ether, air, light, water, earth and time. In Egypt, for example, the Egyptian gods Nun and Naunet were associated with water, Amen and Amaunet with invisibility, Heh and Hauhet with infinity and Kek and Kauket with darkness. Chronos in the Greek pantheon was associated with time, Uranus with the sky, Gaia with the Earth, Nyx with the night and Ananke with a person's destiny.

These gods were not born but are said to have emerged directly from heaven and earth. In Egyptian cosmology, four pairs of deities, the "Ogdoad", were born of the cosmic egg. In Greece, the "Protogenoi" are the first beings that came into existence at the beginning of our universe, from which all of the other gods descend. They include Chaos, Phanes, Physis, Erebus, Nyx, Anake, Chronos and Gaia. In Sumeria they were called Apsu and Tiamat, Anshar and Kishar and Lahmu and Lahamu. In India, this group of gods were called the "Prajapati". They were ten in number. The Dogon, a tribe from West Africa, identify eight primordial beings. They were called the Nommo.

We know the names of two of these beings in Mayan cosmology; it is from these beings that our origin begins. They were called Ometecuhtli and Omecihuatl. We find a similar situation in Polynesia where we only know of one pair of their originating gods. They were called as Rangi and Papa, the Sky Father and Earth Mother. Through their union all of the gods and all living things on the Earth were produced.

One unique feature of this early pantheon of gods is that they are traditionally represented in the form of snakes, as a half man, half snake or some variation of reptilian creature such as a fish, a frog or dragon. The male primordial gods in Egypt, the Ogdoad, are depicted as being frogs or having frog heads. The female

Ogdoad are shown as snakes or having snake heads. In the Sumerian culture, Apsu and Tiamat and Lahmu and Lahamu were snakes.

The dual nature exhibited by the gods has lead some scholars to believe that these early inhabitants of our universe were hermaphrodites. (While I am conjecturing here as to the thoughts of the scholars, if these gods were hermaphrodites it would also imply that they believed that these gods lived at one time and were not just names our ancestors used to refer to natural phenomena.) The word hermaphrodite is formed when you combine the name of Hermes, the great messenger of the gods and Aphrodite, the Greek goddess of love. It is thought to represent the union of the masculine and feminine aspects of God.

This dual nature of the gods is reiterated when you examine the creation stories that come from China. Their legends tell us that the cosmic egg was filled with "opposing principals". The concept of opposing principals is still represented in China and the east as the Yin and Yang - two separate forces united as one. The hermaphroditic nature of the earlier gods is also supported in Japan. In the oldest chronicle of life in Japan, the "*Kojiki*" or the *Record of Ancient Matters*, we are told that the first three deities to appear on the scene were genderless while the five that followed came into being as male-female pairs.

The mythology of the African tribe, the Dogon support the concept of the cosmic egg and the people who came to the Earth in our distant past. The Dogon are a group of people who live in the African nation of Mali in and around the Bandigara Cliff. Their mythology tells us that in the beginning their original creator god Amma created a cosmic egg. Their primordial ancestors, their progenitors were called the Nommo, the Masters of Waters. They were seen as a group of bisexual water gods and are described as amphibious, fish-like creatures. Folk art depictions of the Nommos show creatures with humanoid upper torsos and a fish-like lower torso similar to mermen and mermaids.

91

The Nommo are said to have descended from heaven to Earth in a cosmic egg. This cosmic egg is sometimes referred to as an ark. It was equipped with all of the necessary conditions for life here on Earth. The Dogon believe that the Nommo came to the Earth from the star Digitaria (Sirius B) and began civilization many thousands of years ago. Digitaria, or Sirius B, is a star that orbits the "Dog Star" Sirius in the night sky.

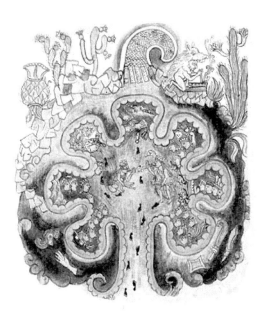

Figure 3: Chicomoztoc, the origin place of the Aztec

Similar legends are found among the Indians of Central America and Mexico. Their creation stories are documented on monuments, stelae and within their written codices. Spanish clergy, beginning in the early 1500's, also recorded their unbelievable myths and legends. One such report comes from Bernardino de Sahagun. Bernardino de Sahagun spent more than 50 years conducting interviews with the Aztec where he explored their beliefs, culture and history. In his *Historia General de las Cosas de Nueva Espana,* Bernardino reported that the first settlers came from the "Chicomoztoc", the "Place of seven Caves" (see figure 3).

The symbolism of the seven caves has been interpreted to mean the seven boats the settlers traveled in. It has also been interpreted as meaning the seven galleys or caves within one enclosure. The Chicomoztoc is also identified as the vehicle(s) *"in which the first settlers of this land came"*.

Diane Wirth (Wirth, 2006) tells us: *"some accounts claim they emerged into a new world from another land, while others refer to their arrival in the world at the time of our present creation"*. She goes on to state that *"Stelae 3 and 6 at Izapa give representations of boats illustrated as U shaped elements. In each case the boat is in the air..."*

Pedro Sarmiento De Gamboa, writing in 1572, recounts that the first Inca (Lords) emerged from a hill called Tampu-tocco, which means "house of windows". The hill was comprised of three windows which were called Maras-tocco, Sutic-tocco and Ccapac-tocco. From the window called Maras-tocco, a tribe called the Maras emerged. Another tribe, called the Tampus, emerged from the window called Sutic-tocco. From the chief window called Ccapac-tocco, which means "the rich window", came four men and four women. They were created by Virachocha and are said to be without parentage. They had been created to be the Lord or Inca of the land.

The Chocktaw people of Tennessee and Mississippi relate a very interesting story. They tell a tale of how all of the people, the birds, the animals and the insects were initially encased in cocoons with their eyes closed and their limbs held in close to their bodies.

David Adams Leeming (Leeming, 1990) shares this version of Creation as told by the Hopi Indians from the Southwestern United States. According to the Hopi:

In the beginning there were only two: Tawa, the Sun God, and Spider Woman, Kokyanwuhti, the Earth Goddess. All the mysteries and the powers in the Above belonged to

Tawa, while Spider Woman controlled the magic of the Below. There was neither man nor woman, bird nor beast, no living thing until these Two willed it to be.

In time they decided there should be other gods to share their labors. So, Tawa divided himself and there came Muiyinwuh, God of All Life Germs and Spider Woman divided herself and there came Huzruiwuhti, Woman of the Hard Substances (turquoise, silver, coral, shell,etc.). Huzruiwuhti became the wife of Tawa and with him produced Puukonhoya, the Youth, and Palunhoya, the Echo, and later, Hicanavaiya, Man-Eagle, Plumed Serpent and many others.

Then did Tawa and Spider Woman have the Great Thought, they would make the Earth to be between the Above and the Below... Spider Woman called all the people so created to follow where she led. Through all the Four Great Caverns of the Underworld she led them, until they finally came to an opening, a sipapu, which led to the earth above... - The World of Myth - David Adams Leeming

Another and probably most shocking reference came from a very unlikely place. It was found in an article published by the *Journal of Cuneiform Studies*. The article was entitled *Antediluvian Cities*. We referenced this article in Chapter 4: *Who Art In Heaven*. *Antediluvian Cities* was written by William W. Hallo a professor of Assyriology and Babylonian Literature at Yale University. The focus of Hallo's article revolved around the establishment of early Sumerian cities. The following astonishing excerpt was contained within the article.

The reptiles verily descend
The earth verily makes its ... (breast?) appear resplendent
It is the garden, it is the foundation-terrace
(Which) the earth-hole for its part fills with water

An (Heaven) is the lord, he is stationed like a young hero
Heaven and Earth cry out together
At that time Enki and Eridu had not appeared
Enlil did not exist
Ninlil did not exist
Brightness was dust
Vegetation was dust
The daylight did not shine
The moonlight did not emerge.
- Antediluvian Cities - William W. Hallo

Hallo, informs us that he is paraphrasing a fragment of a Sumerian text, which was translated by J.J.A. van Dijk. This inscription is said to be one of, if not the oldest known pieces of Sumerian mythology. Intriguing as it is, we have been unable to locate the source of this text other than its reference in Hallo's article. We decided to include it here not only because of what it says, but because of the credentials of the author. They provide veracity for its originality and content.

What are our ancestors telling us? Did the gods, as myth suggests, come from another world? Did they travel to the Earth inside great ships whose description has come down to us a cosmic egg? Are the progenitors the founders of our world and the creators of the human race?

The Progenitors

The retelling of our history commences in what is called the "First World", "Sun" or "Age". The gods, who fill this early pantheon, as well as the later ones, were prodigious, fathering long lines of decedents. The stories that come down to us follow a singular lineage of this vast group of gods, the line of rulership. Even with only one line of the family tree being followed, it is challenging to keep track of who fathered whom. At times the lineage is virtually impossible to determine. Incest was a common practice among the gods. Brothers' marrying sisters or even mothers marrying their sons was not considered taboo. Relationships such as these could explain some of the confusion associated with a god's pedigree.

The other progenitor gods also had children who play pivotal roles in this cosmic drama. The gods who were born outside of the royal line were considered "lesser" gods or were viewed upon as gods of a lower rank or lesser political power. It was only a matter of time, like the dynamics in any dysfunctional family, before the different families began to vie for control.

Some myths indicate that instead of a direct decent from "father to son", as already suggested, each succeeding generation of gods actually represents a usurping race of gods who took charge. The possibility that we are dealing with multiple warring races is made evident in Hindu cosmology.

When we examine the gods in the Hindu tradition, first introduced in chapter 4, we find that Indra (Sakra) was the descendent of Dyaus Pita, the Sky Father and Prithvi, the Earth Mother. Varuna and Yama were the descendents of Daksha and

Prasuti. Daksha and Prasuti were Prajapati - creative principles that were represented as snakes and were associated with fertility and the primordial waters. Finally, we discover that Kubera (Vaisravana) was the grandson of Pulastya who was yet another Prajapati. Pulastya sired the Rakshasas a race of monsters who were associated with treasures and metalworking.

This division by race and not ancestry is also supported in the Nordic tradition. The Eddas describe a world filled with a number of different races. These races include the Aesir and the Vanir. The Vanir were a group of gods associated with fertility, while the Aesir were allied with the sky. The Eddas also include a group of monster gods, which consists of three separate races, the Light Elves, the Dwarves and the Giants.

These unrelated groups of gods, to support their claim of authority, may have identified themselves as the sons and daughters of a preceding race of gods. This practice is attested to in the Old Testament. It was customary for the ancient kings of Israel to claim to be a direct descendant of King David. This relationship validated their authority to rule over Israel. We find the same tradition occurring in England as late as the 15th century AD. The Tudor dynasty of England began when King Henry VII claimed descent from an ancient royal lineage. While Henry's claim was somewhat tenuous, it helped to legitimize his right to the English throne.

Our research into our mythic past reveals three well-established "generations", the originating primordial gods, their children and their grandchildren or the primordial gods and two usurping races. These shifts in rulership loosely parallel the different ages, worlds, suns or epochs in time. These are points in time when the seat of power shifted from one individual or group to another. It is by these generational lines that our story will be unfolding. It is by these generational lines that we find consistency in the stories being told. They also act as markers in our ongoing development of the history of our world.

The First World is clearly recognizable by a number of key elements. This period commences with the arrival of the progenitors onto a dark world or a world characterized as being without a sun, moon or stars. The progenitors were the ruling class of gods during this age. They are identified as being the originators and creators of our universe. The progenitor gods fostered or created a race of beings. This newly formed race rebelled against their creator gods and ultimately took control over the heavens and Earth. This epoch came to its tragic end, according to some legends, when a giant flood destroyed all but a few living beings.

Starting with Babylonian Creation Myth, the *Enuma Elish (When on High . . .)* this is how their story goes.

When on high the heaven had not been named,
Firm ground below had not been called by name,
When primordial Apsu, their begetter,
And Mummu-Tiamat, she who bore them all,
Their waters mingled as a single body,
No reed hut had sprung forth, no marshland had appeared,
None of the gods had been brought into being,
And none bore a name, and no destinies determined--
Then it was that the gods were formed in the midst of heaven.
Lahmu and Lahamu were brought forth,
by name they were called.

Before they had grown in age and stature,
Anshar and Kishar were formed, surpassing the others.
Long were the days, then there came forth.....
Anu was their heir, of his fathers the rival;
Yes, Anshar's first-born, Anu, was his equal.
- Enuma Elish

The *Enuma Elish* provides us with a glimpse of the progenitors of this early world. Here we are introduced to our initiating primordial gods Apsu and Tiamat and Lahmu and Lahamu. It is believed that these originating gods were genderless or hermaphroditic in nature. The next group of god presented,

99

Anshar and Kishar appear to have been created as a male and female pair. Anshar is referred to as the Paternal God of the Sky and the Horizon while Kishar represents the Earth. From their union Anu was born. It is through the lineage of Anu that our story continues.

The *Enuma Elish* goes on to tell us that these early gods were apparently a rowdy bunch. Their behavior disturbed the heavens and the mother of all the gods Tiamat. Apsu tried to calm down his children and grandchildren but was unsuccessful. In an effort to appease Tiamat, he offered to destroy all of the gods so that quiet could be restored. This did not sit well with Tiamat who went into a rage at the thought of losing all of her children. Apsu decided to continue with his dastardly plan to eliminate his progeny. He enlisted the help of his advisor, the god Mummu, the god of knowledge, technical skill and craftsmanship.

Apsu's plans were somehow discovered and soon all of the other gods knew his intent. The gods were reluctant to rise up against Apsu, that is except for Ea (Enki). Ea, the all-wise, saw through Apsu's plan and devised one of his own. Ea, using a spell, put Apsu and Mummu into a deep sleep. Once they were asleep, he tore the tiara off Apsu's head and put it on himself. Then, in a final act of revenge, he slew Apsu. Once his triumph was secured, he established his dwelling upon (on top of) the "Apsu", the watery abyss. The taking of control by Ea marks the end of the First World as well as the end of the reign of the progenitor gods.

We will come back to the narrative provided in the *Enuma Elish* as we continue developing our story. The account of usurpation, of a son violently taking control away from his father, is also described in Greek Mythology in the story of Uranus and Cronus.

The rulers of the cosmos in Greek Mythology were the Protogenoi Uranus the Sky Father and Gaia the Earth Mother. Together they conceived a vast number of giant children who are referred to as the Titans. Their first group of children were the Cyclopes, the one-eyed giants, Brontes, Steropes and Arges. They are described as being great in strength and mighty in the crafts. Their next group of offspring was the "Hecatonchires". The Hecatonchires are described as having 100 hands and 50 heads. Their names were Cottus, Briareos and Gyges.

Uranus hated his Titan sons and locked them up in the depths of the Earth in a place called Tartarus. Tartarus can be found in the underworld or the lowest reaches of the world, in a place void of light. This incensed Gaia who incited her other sons to rebel. The rebellious group was lead by Cronus. Cronus was the youngest son of Uranus and Gaia. Remarkably, unlike his Titan brothers, no physical description of Cronus survives.

Gaia, in support of her children's uprising, gave Cronus an adamantine sickle to use to do the dirty deed. The brothers then laid an ambush for their father. When Uranus attempted to have relations with Gaia they held him down and Cronus, using the sickle, castrated him. The renegade group then took control, liberated their brothers from the depths of Tartarus and raised Cronus to the throne. What happens to Cronus after he takes the throne you will discover as our story continues to unfold. The seizing of power by Cronus from Uranus, like the story of Apsu and Ea, indicates the end of this first epoch.

A tale similar to the story of Uranus and Cronus comes to us from Western Australia. During the "Dream Time" (Altjeringa), a sacred era in which the ancestral spirits lived, the Wati Kutjara traveled all over the western desert. The Wati Kutjara are described as two young lizard men. One story of their exploits informs us that they caught the Moon god, Kidili, trying to rape some of the first women on Earth. Fighting started between Kidili and the Wati Kutjara. One of the Wati Kutjara ended up castrating Kidili with his boomerang. Kidili died in a watering hole and the women he was trying to rape were transformed into the Pleiades.

Legends from the Americas offer a slightly different perspective on the events that transpired during this period. The *Legend Of Viracocha*, as told by Pedro Sarminento De Gamboa, characterizes the essence of the First World of the Inca. Gamboa tells us that in the First World Viracocha created a world without a sun, moon or stars. He also created a race of disproportionately large giants (Titans?). Viracocha wanted the giants to live without quarreling. They were also instructed how to serve Viracocha properly. The giants kept the laws of Viracocha for a while but over time, they sinned and became prideful and contentious. Viracocha, upset by their transgressions cursed them. The Earth swallowed some of the giants. Others were swallowed up by the sea. Then a flood came over the land and drowned all of the created things. Only a few escaped and went on to repopulate the Earth.

Myths from around the world seem to indicate that the gods wished to be "worshiped". Failure to comply with the will of the gods resulted in death and destruction. Today, when we hear the word worship, we commonly imagine going to a church or temple, saying a quiet prayer or in some way communicating with, or exalting god. Is this what the ancient writers were implying? Could the lack of veneration by the giants have led to their complete and ultimate annihilation?

The Hebrew bible, the Torah, offers a clue to the motives of the gods. The word "shehhah", in Hebrew, means "worship" when translated into English. Shehhah, when looked at from an ancient literary point of view had a different meaning from our contemporary understanding of the concept of worship. The interpretation of shehhah, in days of old, referred to the act of prostration, of falling down on one's knees in awe and respect. It is associated with complete surrender and obedience. Is that what the ancient gods really wanted, obedience? Based upon the stories provided, that just might be the case.

The Native American tribe, the Lakota, also tell of the heavenly origin of their gods in their creation mythology. The Lakota are part of a confederation of seven related Sioux tribes, the Očhéthi Šakówin or Seven Council Fires. We are told that in the ancient days, once the process of creation had begun, the creator and trickster god Inktomi conspired with the other gods to cause a rift in the heavens between Takushkanshkan, the Sun God, and his wife, the moon. The separation of the

Takushkanshkan his wife has been used to identify the beginning of time. The story goes on to tell us that after the attempted coup, the conspirators were exiled to the Earth.

The Aztec Indians of Central America believed that the sun god Tezcatlipoca ruled the First World. It is said that Tezcatlipoca only managed to become half of a sun and that the world existed in partial darkness. In this world he created a race of giants that were so powerful that it is said that they could lift trees out of the ground with their bare hands. His brother, Quetzalcoatl, jealous of his reign, knocked Tezcatlipoca out of the sky. Tezcatlipoca was furious for being dethroned and demolished the entire world. The overthrow of Tezcatlipoca and the destruction of the world, according to Aztec cosmology, marks the end of the First World.

A story detailing the play-by-play details of the destruction of the First World comes to us from the Mayan *Book of Chilam Balam of Chumayel:*

It was during the Eleventh Ahau Katún when Ah Mucencab came forth and obscured the face of the Heavens [Oxlahun-ti-Ku] . . . It [the eclipse] occurred when the whole Earth began to awaken, but nobody knew what was to happen. Suddenly the Underworld Fires [Bolon-ti-Ku] seized the Heavens, and fire rained down, and ashes descended, and rocks and trees fell down, and wood and stone smashed together. Then the Heavens were seized and split asunder, the face of the Heavens [Oxlahun-ti-Ku] was buffeted back and forth . . . and thrown on its back . . . After that the fatherless, the miserable ones and the widows were all pierced through [the Tizímin and Mani versions say: "torn to pieces"]: they were all living when their hearts were stopped. And they were buried in the sand beneath the waves.

And in one great sudden rush of water their Great Serpent [Canhel] was ravished from the Heavens [Oxlahun-ti-Ku]. The sky fell down and the dry land sank, when the four

*gods, the four Bacabs arose, who had brought about the
annihilation of the world.*
*After the destruction was complete . . . the four pillars of the
sky [Bacab trees] were re-established . . . And the Great
Mother Seiba rose amidst recollections of the destruction of
the Earth.* - Book of Chilam Balam of Chumayel

Some myths state that the four Bacabs escaped the
destruction of the First World and were sent to hold up the four
corners of the sky in the Second World. Not surprisingly, the four
Bacabs are also giants. Their names were Hobnil, Cantzicnal,
Saccimi, and Hosanek.

We know from Norse mythology that Odin, Vili and Ve, the
three sons of the giants' race rebelled against their makers. One of
their acts was to kill their creator god Ymir. The Norse ascribe the
subsequent flood to the killing of Ymir. Accordingly, so much
blood flowed from Ymir's body that it filled the abyss. All of the
giants died except two, Bergelmir and his wife. They escaped in a
small boat and it is from these two survivors that a new race of
giants came forth. The Aesir (gods) then set about repairing the
destruction that was caused by their conflict with the giants. The
word Aesir translates as pillars and supporters of the world.

Hindu tradition tells us that at the end of the last *kalpa*, the
last great cycle, the vedas (the knowledge of creation) were stolen
from Brahma by a power seeking god (an Asura) named
Hayagriva. Hayagriva ran away and hid the vedas in the depths of
the ocean. A similar story tells us that Brahma had became
extremely proud of his position as the creator. Vishnu wanting to
teach him the lesson of humbleness, created two Asuras, Madhu
and Kaitabha, who stole the vedas from Brahma. Madhu and
Kaitabha hid the vedas in the Patala. Patala is often translated as
underworld. Without the knowledge contained within the vedas,
Brahma was unable to continue with his work of creating the
material world.

Lord Vishnu, at the request of Brahma, took the form of the
fish Matsya to retrieve them. Matsya was the first incarnation or

avatar of Vishnu on Earth. An avatar is the essence of Vishnu when he descends upon the Earth and takes on material form. Nine avatars have appeared on the Earth throughout the course time. They have appeared in the form of animals, monsters and men. Matsya is described as having the head and torso of a man. The lower part of his body is said to look like a fish.

The conclusion of the last *kalpa* was quickly approaching. Before it ended, Matsya defeated the Asura and returned the vedas to Brahma. At the same time, to help save humanity, Matsya appeared to the pious sage Satyavrata (Manu). Matsya warned Satyavrata that a great flood, that would inundate the entire universe, was about to occur. He instructed Satyavrata to gather up the seeds, plants and animals needed for rebuilding the next cycle of creation. He was also told to gather up the Sapta Rishis, the seven sages and Vasuki, the great serpent king.

Rain started to fall and the oceans began to rise. A boat appeared to where Satyavrata, Vasuki, and the Sapta Rishi, were waiting. The boat was fastened to Matsya's horn and they sailed throughout the night of Brahma and saved mankind from dissolution.

Stories of a flood that ends the world are traditionally associated with the biblical story of Noah. The story of Matsya is no exception. Many contemporary scholars believe that this flood occurred around 11,700 years ago. Our research into this event shows something we believe many scholars never considered. By looking at what transpired both before the flood and after, stories of a great flood seem to indicate two separate and distinct flood events.

While we are getting ahead of ourselves in our narrative, the flood that ended the First World is clearly recognizable by the events that transpire after the destruction of the world, namely the formation and creation of the Earth. The creation of the Earth will be explored in depth as we move ahead. We believe the creation story provides an irrefutable marker in time and is not associated with the flood event typically allied with Noah. We also believe that the story of the fish Matsya may have been influenced by legends of the second flood leaving us with the tale you have just read.

It is here, at the end of the First World that we hope to clear up the discrepancies between the recollections of cycles of time seen in various cultures. Earlier we spoke of some cultures tracking time in a system of five Suns, Worlds, Ages or Epochs, while others only recount four. Hindu tradition, for example, relates four cycles of time. The first cycle, the first creation, occurred with the appearance of Matsya. Other cultures, as we have just explored, describe a time that existed prior to this massive destruction event.

The concept of two separate beginnings left us with several unanswered questions. The first was, why? Why was there a discrepancy between the beginning of time in the various accounts? Why did some stories chronicle a time before the flood and then others identify the beginning of time as occurring afterwards?

We looked to the Hindu tradition of cycles of time for some possible answers. In the story of Matsya, Matsya appeared at the transition between the previous *kalpa* and the current one some 4 billion years ago. The Earth, when looked at from a geological perspective at this early point in its formation, does not support the mythology of a worldwide flood and its subsequent reconstruction.

Therefore, we thought, what if the place associated with the First World was not the Earth. What if the gods, in their travels through space, arrived somewhere else first? Then, after the catastrophe that caused the destruction of the First World. they came to the Earth and created a new beginning, a new world? This, we reasoned, would explain some of the confusion associated with the various new beginnings we encountered.

The next logical question that came to us was if the gods did not come to Earth, then where did they go? Though this is complete speculation on our part, we would like to propose that the gods arrived on Mars first. Is there any direct evidence in the historical, archeological or mythological record to support this claim? No. Is there, on the other hand, circumstantial evidence or at least some very interesting coincidences that make this a possibility. Yes!

Scientists agree that our solar system was formed around 4.5 billion years ago. In less than 2 million years, even to the astonishment of researchers, Mars' environment was drastically different from what was evolving on the Earth during the same time period. This epoch in Mars' history is called the Noachian Era. Jean-Pierre Bibring (Bibring, 2005) states: *"If we look at today's evidence, the era in which Mars could have been habitable and sustained life would be the early Noachian."* The Noachian Era ended about 3.7 billion years ago.

Mars, according to astrobiologists, was covered with large lakes or oceans. It also possessed an atmosphere and a magnetic field, which protected the planet from harmful radiation. Mars has also been found to have the rudimentary beginning of life - bacterial growth. Mars was well on its way to being an Earth-like planet.

Then catastrophe stuck. Mars, like many of the other planets in our solar system, underwent a period of heavy impact involvement. The planet's crater record indicates that Mars suffered massive impacts in quick succession, which began shortly after the planets' formation and ended about 3.8 billion years ago. The heaviest period of impacts on Mars began about 4.2 billion years ago and is identified as the Late Heavy Bombardment. It is theorized that because of the succession of impacts, and no time for the planet to recover, Mars lost its magnetic field.

Planets such as Earth, Mars and Mercury have or had a magnetic field because of the movement of molten iron inside their cores. Through a process called convection, molten iron rises, cools and sinks within the planet's core, generating an electric current. The spinning of the planet turns that electrical current into a magnetic field. This system is known as the dynamo. When the dynamo died on Mars, it lost its atmosphere and its chance for supporting life.

Amazingly, our fossil record indicates that the first signs of life, simple forms of bacteria, appeared on the earth 3.8 billion years ago. Amir Alexander (Alexander, 2009) comments, *"How life appeared and flourished so suddenly on our planet when the bombardment ended is one of the great scientific mysteries of our time."*

The First World ended and a new beginning arose in the Second World, the "Golden Age". In its wake, we are left with a number of unanswered questions. Could the dimly lit surface of Mars actually be the dark world described in these early legends? Was the astonishing transformation of Mars from a newly formed planet to one that was capable of sustaining life a natural occurrence or was the hand of god involved?

Was the catastrophe that destroyed the First World an environmental nightmare or did something a bit more sinister occur? Could the devastation experienced on the dark world of the first age have been so great that it caused a group of the gods to flee? Was it the rebels, the instigating giants, and their leader, who escaped before the First World was destroyed? Did this rogue group of gods steal the technology used to terraform planets from the progenitor gods? Could the ship directed by Matsya actually be describing the ship that brought this group of individuals from Mars to the Earth? Could the beginning of the current *kalpa*, 4.32 billion years ago reflect the beginnings of a new world after the disaster on the last world?

One last question before we continue. If the gods were directly involved in the creation and formation of the world, who performed the terraforming? We believe the group of lesser gods associated with the God of Treasures, the giants, dwarfs or monsters, would have done this work. Mythology tells us that the giants, the Titans or the dwarfs, depending on the culture, were associated with the "crafts". They were, as you may recall, the ones responsible for building the *sabha's*, the heavenly vessels of the Hindu pantheon. They were also responsible for constructing the magnificent weapons of the gods, such as Zeus' thunderbolt,

108

Poseidon's trident, Odin's spear Gungnir, their fiery chariots as well as their other high technology devices.

Chinese legend says that the god Pan Gu set about the task of creating the world. In the beginning, Pangu slept for over 18,000 years in an egg that existed in total darkness. He cracked the egg open when he awoke. The heavy and light parts of the egg separated creating the heavens and the Earth. Pan Gu, in other legends, created the heavens and Earth with a swing of his giant axe. Pan Gu sometimes appears as a dwarf with two horns on his head. In other legends, he is described as a hairy giant with horns on his head and dressed in furs. He is traditionally shown holding a hammer in one hand and a chisel in the other.

Mayan legend tells us that in the first world a dwarf race of beings, the Saiyamboob "the Adjusters", built cities in the darkness. The Saiyamkoob, when the sun finally appeared turned to stone. It is said that their images, can be "found in the ruins".

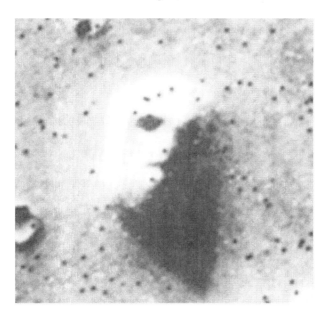

Figure 4: The Face on Mars - Image taken by the
Viking 1 orbiter (Source: NASA/JPL)

Could the highly controversial "Face on Mars" and nearby pyramidal structures in the Cydonia region of Mars actually be remnants of their presence?

The Golden Age

In the last chapter we proposed that a group of gods came to the Earth around 4.32 billion years ago and founded the Second World. A number of key features identify this new era. They include an abundant and prosperous world, a world covered with water and the habitation of subterranean realms by the gods. The gods also created a new race of men during this period. How the Second World ends is something we will delve into later on in our chronology.

The Second World, according to our accounting of time is characterized as being a new beginning - a Golden Age. The concept of a Golden Age can be found in cultures worldwide. In some societies, the Golden Age is considered the First World (Age) and is connected to the beginning of time. First or Second, the Golden Age is acknowledged as being an ideal age, characterized by peace, prosperity, wisdom and virtue. The race of men who lived during this time were free from sorrow or care. The people lived happy and joyous lives. They never suffered the ills of old age nor did they lose their strength. This concept is supported by myths that come to us from the Americas.

The First People knew no sickness. Not until evil entered the world did persons get sick in the body or head... they understood themselves... were pure and happy... they felt as one and understood one another without talking. - Frank Waters, *Book of the Hopi*

In the days of Quetzalcoatl there was abundance of everything necessary for subsistence. The maize was plentiful, the calabashes were as thick as one's arm, and cotton grew in all colours without having to be dyed. A variety of birds of rich plumage filled the air with their songs, and gold, silver, and precious stones were abundant. In the reign of Quetzalcoad there was peace and plenty for all men.
- The Myths Of Mexico And Peru - Lewis Spence

They declare that, in the days of Coniraya Uiracocha, their country was yunca, and that the crops ripened in five days. This is also impossible, for the situation of this province is the same as that of all the country which slopes from the snowy chain of mountains to the sea, from Pasto to Chile, a distance of more than twelve hundred leagues. If this small portion was ever yunca, the whole of the rest of that region which slopes towards the sea must also have been yunca, which the people deny; therefore this district cannot have been so. For there cannot have been a change of climate affecting this small district without breaking the chain of mountains, and then continuing it again, which is absurd. -
A Narrative of the Errors, False Gods, and Other Superstitions and Diabolical Rites in Which the Indians of the Provinces of Huarochri, Mama and Chaclla Lived in Ancient Times, and in Which They Even Now Live, to the Great Perdition of Their Souls - Doctor Francisco de Avila

Dominion during this age was held by the usurping race of gods. Greek tradition informs us that Cronus, having secured a victory over Uranus, re-imprisoned the Giants, the Hecatonkheires and the Cyclops in the depths of Tartarus. The gates of Tartarus were guarded by Campe. Campe is described by Nonnus, in his work *Dionysiaca*, as being part woman, part scale covered sea monster with the tail of a scorpion. Cronus then took his sister Rhea as his wife to rule the world with him. A Golden Age followed.

112

Ea, according to the Sumerian creation myth the *Enuma Elish*, after securing his triumph over his grandfather Apsu, established a dwelling in the watery deep, which he called "Apsu". He was joined in the Apsu by the seven Abgal or Apkallu who were demigods created by the god Ea. The Abgal were described as fish-like men who would emerge periodically from the Apsu. They are represented as having the lower body of a fish and the upper body of a man. In some representations they are shown as being dressed like fish rather than being fish-like themselves.

Dogon legend informs us that the Nommo (who are described as looking remarkably similar to the seven Abgal) came to the Earth via a cosmic egg. The cosmic egg was divided into two twin placentas, which contained four pairs of Nommos. For some reason, one of the Nommo left the egg "before gestation" and came down to Earth through space outside the egg. The remaining seven Nommo followed traveling along a gigantic arch.

Hindu tradition tells us that Matsya the fish saved Satyavrata (Manu) and the seeds of humanity from the devastating flood that marked the end of the last world and cycle of time. The seven Sapta Rishis joined Satyavrata and were saved from this destruction. We do not know what happened to Satyavrata after his arrival but we do know some of the early acts of the gods reported in the Hindu tradition. We will be delving into these acts in the next chapter.

Another feature of the Second World is a world submerged beneath water. It is within this watery world that the gods set up shop. Their palaces and homes, instead of being built on the surface of the Earth, were constructed beneath its land and water.

That's the way the creation of the earth was, when it was formed by the Heart of Heaven, the Heart of the Earth. That's what the first ones who inseminated were called, when heaven was in suspension and the earth was found submerged in the water. - Popol Vuh

The Earth, according to the Babylonian legend the *Fight Between Bel and the Dragon*, was just one vast sea. It is here on this wet world that Ea constructed the first city Eridu. Theophilus Pinches, writing in 1908 suggests that Eridu was not the name of an Earthly city but one that was found within the abyss. The building of the Apsu is described in the Sumerian text *"Enki Builds the E-Engurra"* as being like a mountain and that when Enki "raises" the city of Eridu from the abyss it can float over the water. The Apsu, like the subterranean realms of the gods described earlier, is adorned with silver, lapis lazuli, carnelian and gold. It is portrayed as being the garden of the gods and is said to be filled with fruit bearing trees, birds and animals of all kinds. These plants and animals were sent down from the heavens to the Apsu by the gods.

The subterranean nature of Eridu is supported in the *Epic of Gilgamesh* where Tablet IX of this saga chronicles Gilgamesh's endeavor to meet Utnapishtim the survivor of the great flood. Utnapishtim was said to live beyond Mount Mashu. When Gilgamesh reached Mount Mashu he was greeted by scorpion beings guarding the gates to the netherworld. After gaining entrance, he traveled for eleven leagues in the darkness. When he had traveled a full twelve leagues underground, his surroundings grew bright. He entered a realm filled with animals and fruit bearing trees. It was adorned with lapis lazuli, carnelian, rubies, hematite and emeralds.

The concept of a subterranean abode of the gods is also reflected in the Mayan creation story, the *Popol Vuh*. It recounts that below the sea was a region called Xibalbá that was ruled by two gods called Hun Caquix and Vucub Caquix. Xibalbá or "Place of Fear" is the underworld in Mayan mythology. The entrance to Xibalbá could be found at the mouth of a cave, which was believed to be near Cobán in Guatemala. The passageway into this subterranean habitat of the gods was filled with tests, traps and obstacles that challenged anyone who dared to enter. If one managed to survive its numerous trials he would come upon a

114

large place filled with gardens and a number of structures, including the homes of the gods.

As the story goes, once the Earth had recovered from the wrath of the gods (the flood), the world was ruled by the prideful god of the underworld, Vucub Caquix. Vucub Caquix name means "Seven-times-the-colour-of-fire," or "Very brilliant". The gods were so irritated by Vucub Caquix's prideful nature and boastful ways that they decided to overthrow him. They sent the hero-gods Hun-Ahpu and Xbalanque to eliminate Vucub Caquix and his progeny. We will be going into detail regarding the overthrow of the gods of the Second World shortly.

Yet another characteristic of the Second World was the creation of a new race of man. Aztec mythology tells us that under the rulership of Quetzalcoatl, the god of the Aztec Golden Age, a new group of people were created to inhabit the Earth. It is assumed, in modern times, that the chroniclers are talking about a group of beings just like us. Mythology does not support this view. The group of beings created during the Second World are not represented as appearing in the form we now take for granted as humanity. Perhaps a better way of thinking about these subsequent generations of mankind would be by viewing them as "Earth-born". This would include any group or version of being created or born on the earth, including modern man.

Cronos, for example, created man during his many years reign in heaven. He is said to have watched over his creation like a loving parent. Humankind, during this period, did not live in cities. They are described as living in the open air without clothing. They had no cares, worries, nor any resources or skills. The gods looked upon them as we look at our cat or dog. They lived on the bounty of the Earth. The fruits of the Earth spontaneously sprang up of its own accord during this age providing all of the things necessary for man. There was no need for plowing or sowing, labor or toil.

This new race of man was born of the blood of the castrated Uranus that spilled upon the earth. Greek tradition refers to them as the Giants, the Erinyes (Furies) and the Meliae (nymphs of the manna ash tree). The giants, fashioned upon this world, are much smaller than the Titans who were created in the previous age. They are described as being somewhere between eight and ten feet in height. The Titans, on the other hand are reported as enormous, with some texts describing them as being as big as a mountain.

The Norse poem, the *Völuspá*, tells us that the dwarfs were created from the primordial blood of Brimir and the bones of Bláinn. The *Prose Edda*, in turn describes the dwarfs as having been formed from maggots that fed on the body of their creator god Ymir. The dwarfs are also described as beings that live within the Earth and beneath its mountains. They are associated with wisdom, mining, metal smithing and the crafts.

Four of the seven Dogon gods, the Nommo, after their arrival on Earth took up positions at the cardinal points of the Earth (North, South, East and West). This concept is reminiscent of the four Bacabs. They were the giants of the Mayan pantheon who escaped the destruction of the First World and went on to hold up the sky in the Second. Dogon cosmology goes on to inform us that these four Nommo gave birth to the four tribes, the Arou, the Dyon, the Ono and the Domno. The remaining two Nommo took on the role of blacksmiths and ironworkers. They are described as mighty in the crafts like the Cyclopes and dwarfs.

Not everything transpired below ground during the Second World. Above ground, on the surface of the Earth, new life (bacteria) had miraculously appeared. Lewis Spence (Spence, 1913) claims that the natives of the New World believed that the Earth was created from "slime" that rose above the primeval waters. García Ordóñez de Montalvo in his *Origin de los Indias* writes:

In the year and in the day of the clouds, before ever were years or days, the world lay in darkness. All things were orderless, and a water covered the slime and ooze that the earth then was. - *Origin de los Indias* - García Ordóñez de Montalvo

Scientists agree that it is from these very simple early organisms that the diversity of life on Earth evolved.

The Arunta Tribe of Australia provide this very enigmatic tale that fits remarkably well into this time period. During the Alcheringa or dreamtime of the Arunta, the world was covered with salt water. In the western sky two beings emerged. These beings were said to be Ungambikula. They were self-existent or came out of nothing. When they arrived on the Earth they found masses of incomplete plants, animals and humans beings (Inapertwa). They were formless creatures who dwelt in groups along the shores of the salty sea. Using their Lalira or great stone knives, the Ungambikula began their task of creating men and women. It required many years of working with their stone knives for the Ungambikula to form a human being out of the native Inapertwa.

First of all the arms were released, then the fingers were added by making four clefts at the end of each arm; then legs and toes were added in the same way. The figure could now stand, and after this the nose was added and the nostrils bored with the fingers. A cut with the knife made the mouth, which was pulled open several times to make it flexible. A slit on each side separated the upper and lower eye-lids, hidden behind which the eyes were already present, another stroke or two completed the body, and thus, out of the Inapertwa, men and women were formed. - The Native Tribes of Central Australia - Baldwin Spencer and F. J. Gillen

Did the renegade gods come to the Earth and create a new world, a new beginning? What was their purpose in doing so? Stay tuned as we explore the first acts of the gods here on Earth.

117

The Fight For Immortality

The biggest mystery associated with the gods is why they came here in the first place. There are a variety of theories as to why an advanced civilization would come to the Earth. The one that often surfaces is that there were problems on their home world such as overpopulation, pollution or a shortage of natural resources. These issues could have caused a group of explorers to leave their planet and "seek out new life and new civilizations". It could be that their home world was destroyed and a lucky few managed to escape. Perhaps the "Galactic Federation of Planets" needed to create a way station between heaven (Asgard) and hell (Hel). It does seem apparent from ancient sources that the subjugation of humankind was NOT their goal. Whew...That is a relief.

The truth is we really fall short on the why side of things. One thing we do have is some insight into was the activities of the gods when they first came to the Earth during the Second World. Their actions, as you will see, make them look anything but holy or God-like. Our story continues...

We know from mythology that a great flood covered the Earth. Land reclamation has yet to happen. Water from the flood, according to Hindu tradition, took away many of their "precious things" and one of the most precious things lost by the gods was something called "amrita".

What is amrita? It was the drink of the gods, the elixir of life, the nectar of immortality. The word amrita is a Sanskrit word meaning immortality or "without death". Ambrosia is the Greek name for this divine blend. The consumption of this magical potion was reserved for divine beings - the gods. Mortals, such as Heracles, who was provided ambrosia gained immortality. Gilgamesh, in the Babylonian epic bearing his name, tied heavy stones to his feet so that he would be taken down into the depths of the water to reclaim a plant called "The Old Man Becomes a Young Man". The Old Man Becomes a Young Man, when eaten, bestowed youth.

Indian tradition suggests that during this time the different races of gods banded together into two separate alliances - the Devas and the Asuras. The word Deva originally meant celestial or shinning one. They are described as the "good gods". The Asuras, on the other hand, are portrayed as being evil, power-seeking, sinful and materialistic. The Devas are traditionally depicted as looking like us while the Asuras are shown in the form of snakes, demons and monsters. A truce was called, in the wake of the flood, and these two groups reluctantly joined forces in order to recover their precious amrita from the watery depths. It is from our watery world that the plot thickens.

In the legend of the *Churning of the Milky Ocean* we learn that the Devas were losing their power and started to feel threatened by the might of the Asuras. War inevitably broke out between the two groups. The Devas feared that the Asuras would win and take control of the entire world. They prayed to the god Vishnu for guidance. Vishnu suggested that the gods (the Devas) perform the ceremony known today as the Churning of the Ocean. This would enable them to obtain their beloved amrita and help to restore their power. Despite this sage advice, the Devas realized that they were not strong enough to perform the ceremony by themselves. They enlisted the help of the Asuras under the pretext that they would mutually share the amrita.

The story goes on to tell us that they took Mount Mandara and used it as a rod to churn the ocean. The Devas and Asuras were unable to find a rope big enough to go around the mountain so they enlisted the help of the King of the Nagas (serpents) Vasuki. Vasuki was wound around the mountain with the Devas in the East and the Asuras in the west. Each side pulled on the snake alternately causing the mountain to rotate. The churning caused Mount Mandara to sink into the ocean. Vishnu, in his second incarnation on Earth, magically appeared as Kurma the tortoise. Kurma went to the bottom of the ocean and Mount Mandara was placed on his back. Churning operations continued.

The Devas and Asuras churned the ocean for a thousand years. Suddenly, a deadly poison called halahala emerged, some say from the ocean, others say from Vasuki himself. The poison threatened to suffocate both the Devas and Asuras. Only the god Shiva could save them from this potential disaster. Shiva, trident in hand, arrived on the scene in the nick of time. He drank the noxious poison and rescued the Devas and Asuras from their likely demise.

The gods continued churning the milky ocean even longer, then out of the ocean sprang a number of gifts. They included Sura (the goddess and creator of wine), the Apsaras (the heavenly nymphs), Kasthuba (the most valuable jewel in the world), Uchhaishravas (the divine horse), Parijata (the wish-granting tree), Kamadhenu (the first cow and mother of all other cows) and Lakshmi (the Goddess of Fortune and Wealth). The final gift to emerge was Dhanavantri, the Heavenly Physician, with a pot containing their precious amrita. We will be coming back to this story as we continue our journey through time.

The Rig Veda refers to amrita as soma as well, but as we will explore, amrita and soma may be two different substances. Greek texts distinguish two different foods of the god, ambrosia and nectar. Ambrosia is described as something that is eaten, while nectar is a beverage that is drunk.

Soma, or Soma Ras (juice of soma) is well described in the Rig Veda. The word soma comes from the root word "su" and suggests the concept of pressing or pounding. Soma is touted for its ability to allow the gods to rise above all obstacles and overcome their fears. It is said to bring about hallucinations and feelings of ecstasy to those who drink it. It can also help to create a bridge between the mortal world and the worlds of the gods. Soma is associated with the moon and is said to help promote inspiration and the creative process. The Rig Veda calls soma the "master poet".

Its prominence in Indian society even elevated this substance to god status, placing soma in a position higher than Indra himself. Texts indicate that soma is created when the stalks of the soma plant are pounded between two rocks. The golden-hued liquid that is released by the stalks is filtered through wool and collected. The juice is then mixed with other ingredients including water, milk and barley and is said to taste similar to honey.

The identity of the plant used in making soma is a mystery. Robert Gordon Wasson (Wasson, 1972) speculates that it was made from juices of the psychoactive mushroom, Amanita Muscaria. Consumption of this mushroom can create feelings of euphoria, hallucinations as well as feelings of increased strength and stamina.

Wasson cited the red color of the mushroom as an indicator of its relationship with the god Soma. He goes on to propose that texts contained within the *Mahabharata* indicate the likelihood of his identification. The *Mahabharata* tells the story of the holy man Uttanka. Uttanka was traveling through the desert and was thirsty. He met an outcast who offered him some of his urine to drink. Disgusted, Uttanka refused. Uttanka was later told by Krishna (a later incarnation of Vishnu) that the outcast had offered him Soma-urine. Had he accepted it, he would have joined the immortals.

The account of Uttanka further supported Wasson's hypothesis that Amanita Muscaria was the most likely candidate. The active ingredients in the Amanita muscaria mushroom, unlike other hallucinogens, passes through the kidneys unmetabolized. The urine that is expelled by the ingester has been found to be as potent as the mushroom itself.

Another possibility as to the composition of soma comes to us from recent discoveries in Russia. Excavations in the Kara Kum desert of Turkmenistan has provided evidence that soma may actually have been a combination of cannabis and ephedra or cannabis, ephedra and poppy. Bowls found in one room of the site were analyzed showing traces of both cannabis and ephedra. Both of these plants were found growing in and around the area of the excavation. In another room, vessels that were used to prepare the drink were discovered. Small amounts of cannabis, ephedra and poppy were recovered from the sides of the pots and pitchers.

In Persia, we find a similar brew called "hoama" which played a role in Zoroastrian doctrines. The *Avesta*, a collection of Zoroatrian sacred texts, informs us that hoama had to be pressed to extract its intoxicating juices. Its effects upon consumption of this plant included: healing, sexual arousal, increased physical strength and mental alertness. It is also described as being mildly intoxicating. The ephedra plant is believed to have been used to manufacture hoama in this region.

Soma is most often aligned with the Greek's nectar. The word nectar comes from the Greek word nektar, which means "drink of the gods". Some historians claim that nectar was a kind of honey or fermented honey wine but its connection to immortality is vague. The difference between amrita and soma and ambrosia and nectar does become clear to us when we visit Norse mythology.

In Norse tradition, there is a distinction between the substances that were ingested to obtain immortality verses wisdom. Immortality, according to this tradition is associated with golden apples. The Mead of Poetry (skáldskapar mjaðar), on the other hand, is tied to the concept of the attainment of wisdom and poetic inspiration.

Norse legend tells us that a truce was established between the Aesir (the Gods of War) and the Vanir (the Gods of Fertility) after their great war. Both groups, disgusting as this sounds, spat into a vat to seal their truce. From their saliva Kvasir was born. Kvasir was a very wise man who traveled the world giving knowledge to humankind. One day he paid a visit to the dwarves Fjalar and his brother Galar. The dwarves killed Kvasir and poured his blood into two vats. They mixed his blood with honey, thus creating "mead". Anyone who drank the mead was endowed with wisdom and the power of poetry. The story goes on and we find that the giants, after a series of unfortunate events, end up getting the mead as reparation from the dwarfs. Odin, the head of the Aesir pantheon, through an act of trickery, turned around and stole the mead from the giants; taking it back to Aesir and sharing it with the other gods.

The story of the Mead Of Poetry on the surface may not appear to reveal the relationship between the Hindu concept of soma and the mead of the Norse. Dustin Tranberg (Tranberg, 1992) ties the two together.

The Vedic soma and the "mead of poetry" found in the Prose Edda, share several qualities. For example, both are connected to the idea of "pressing," as of pressing the juice from a fruit. In the hymns of the Rig Veda, soma is pressed out in to bowls. The Icelandic Skaldskaparmal tells of the manufacture of the mead of poetry from the blood of a being named Kvasir, whose name "has often been associated with Danish 'kvase' (to squeeze to extract juice)... - Soma And The Mead Of Poetry - Dustin Tranberg

The Maya of Central America also utilized a mead-like substance with intoxicating properties. It was called Balche and was sacred to the gods. It was made by soaking the bark of the Balche Tree (L. Violaceus) in honey and water.

It is impossible to determine the exact composition of this mysterious drink. What has been passed down to us is that the gods are often portrayed as competing with each other for this intoxicating brew. Indra was a big fan of soma as was the Hindu god of Fire, Agni. Odin went so low as to steal it from the giants who managed to get it away from the dwarfs, who got it by killing Kvasir. It seems like everyone wanted to have it for themselves.

It does seem clear from the ancient accounts that soma, nectar, skáldskapar mjaðar, and balche were all drinks that caused intoxication. It is also clear that the substances of these drinks did not come from the depths of the milky ocean as descried earlier but were herbal in nature.

So, what were the Devas and Asuras drilling for in the ocean? It must have been more important to them than soma, considering the number of years they spent churning the ocean to possess it. To help us identify what it may have been, we believe that a likely candidate may come from a system of values that we inherited from our distant past.

If you look around the world, countless doctrines and beliefs have shaped our society. They have no clear or rational purpose. They only make sense in one context: that they were important, real or of value to the gods. We in turn follow these traditions either because we did not know any better or because we had a strong desire to emulate the gods.

Take for example our concept of heaven. Have you ever wondered why there is a widespread belief that God, with a big "G", lives in Heaven. Where is Heaven? Is it located up in the sky. Likewise, there is the corresponding belief that the dead, or sometimes the wicked, go to a place deep within (or beneath) the Earth. This place was reportedly inhabited by demons. Are we just stating something that was point and fact? Did the gods live in, or come from, the sky? Did demons live underground, deep within the Earth sometime in our distant past?

The tradition of worshiping a ruler as a god also falls into this category. The Egyptians, like many early cultures around the world, perceived their rulers as gods or sometimes direct decedents of the gods. Could this tradition have been passed onto us because in the earliest of times the pharaoh or ruler was actually a god or demi-god?

The cultural tradition of the deformation of cranial bones is yet another example. Cranial deformation (head flattening) is a practice found in South America, Australia, Europe and China. It is thought to be an indicator of increased intelligence, higher social status and a closer relationship to the spiritual world. Did these cultures practice cranial deformation because they were emulating the physical appearance of their gods? Did dogma prevail? Did the now mortal rulers, who took over after the reign of the gods, try to fool the population into believing that they too

125

were gods? Did the descendants of the faux gods accidently turn cranial deformation into an essential requirement of royalty thereby following a tradition they did not understand?

References to the importance and value of gold are echoed in mythology worldwide. It, over any other material found on the Earth, has been a symbol of wealth, social standing and power throughout time. Nations have fought and died over it. Legends of lost cities of gold and hidden treasures pervade our culture. But why?

Gold, by nature, is a soft dense metal. It is extremely malleable and has to be mixed with other base metals in order to increase its hardness. Other than its bright yellow color and shiny luster, it seems odd that the ancients would go to such extreme lengths for this metal if its only purposes were for making coins, jewelry and works of art.

We still relish and prize gold for its intrinsic qualities. Its primary use is in the manufacture of ornamental objects such as jewelry. Today, in our high-tech world, we recognize and utilize the phenomenal inherent properties gold offers. We use ultra-thin sheets of it to reflect infrared radiation on spacecraft and spacesuits. Its non-corrosive and highly conductive properties also make it an excellent choice in the electronics industry. Assuming that the Egyptians, Sumerians and people of ancient Peru were not manufacturing cell phones, computers or heat shields, it still leaves us with the question as to why gold was and is valued so highly. My response is we value it because it was important to the gods.

We know from the story of the *Churning of the Milky Ocean* that the gods sought out the life restoring properties that amrita offered. We know that immortality was conferred upon the Greek gods and mortals who consumed ambrosia. Accordingly, humans who ate ambrosia grew faster, stronger, and more beautiful. These were all qualities that were considered divine. Eating ambrosia also endowed humans with immortality.

Today recipes for ambrosia call for fruit that is sweetened with sugar, marshmallow or honey. Is our modern concept of

126

ambrosia supported by mythology? We do find some collaboration in mythology as to the nature of amrita, ambrosia, immortality and gold. Norse mythology provides us with two separate clues. The first comes from the *Voluspa*, a poem in the Poetic Edda. The *Voluspa* recalls the war between the Aesir and the Vanir. We have already discussed the conclusion of this battle when we talked about the Mead of Poetry earlier in this chapter. The cause of the war, however, was a fight over gold.

The Nordic poem, the *Voluspa*, informs us that war broke out between the Aesir, the Sky Gods and Vanir, the Fertility Gods, after the Aesir tortured the Vanir goddess, Gullveig. The Aesir burned Gullveig three times in a magical fire, only to have Gullveg come back to life. The Vanir were miffed. The Vanir, in reparation for the Aesir's ill treatment of Gullveig, demanded status equal to the Aesir. The Aesir refused and instead waged war against the Vanir. Unfortunately, the war did not go as well as the Aesir had hoped. The Aesir suffered defeat after defeat and finally, to save face, arranged for a truce. Both groups spat into a vat and the Mead of Poetry was created.

In case you were wondering, the entomology of the name Gullveig also adds support to the claim that gold was associated with immortality. The first part of the name Gullveig, *Gul*, means "gold". The second part, *veig*, has two potential meanings. Both meanings make sense in the context we are offering. The word v*eig* is sometimes translated as "alcoholic drink". At other times it is translated as "power" or "strength".

The second source coming from Norse mythology is connected to the goddess Iðunn, the goddess of eternal youth. Iðunn was the keeper and protector of the magical golden apples we mentioned earlier. Consuming these apples allowed the gods to maintain their eternal youthfulness.

Now, these apples were the fruit of a magic tree, and were more beautiful to look at and more delicious to taste than any fruit that ever grew. The best thing about them was that whoever tasted one, be he ever so old, grew young and strong again. The apples belonged to a beautiful lady named Iðunn, who kept them in a golden casket. Every morning the Aesir came to her to be refreshed and made over by a bite of her precious fruit. That is why in Asgard no one ever waxed old or ugly. Even Father Odin, Hoenir, and Loki, the three travelers who had seen the very beginning of everything, when the world was made, were still sturdy and young. And so long as Iðunn kept her apples safe, the faces of the family who sat about the table of Valhalla would be rosy and fair like the faces of children. – The Days Of Giants; A Book Of Norse Tales - Abbie Farwell Brown

Another legend revolving around golden apples comes to us from Greek mythology where we learn about the Garden of the Hesperides. The Hesperides were nymphs who looked after a garden, which was located in the far western corner of the world. In one section of their garden, Hera, Zeus' wife, planted a tree that bore golden apples. These apples, when consumed, also conferred immortality.

A similar life giving fruit can be found in Chinese mythology. Legend holds that certain peach trees were endowed with mystical virtues that bestowed longevity on those who were lucky enough to taste them. The trees were located high on top of the mountains of K'un-lun in Hsi Wang Mu's, the Goddess of Immortality's palace. The trees are said to put forth leaves once every three thousand years. It would take another three thousand years for the fruits on the tree to ripen. A large banquet was held for the gods once the fruits had matured. All of the gods would attend and consume the fruit and thus their immortality would be restored. This event was called the Festival of Peaches.

The consumption of both a food and a beverage as the source of immortality are echoed in the Sumerian tale of *Adapa and the Food of Life*. Adapa was the mortal, although powerful son of the god Ea. One day, while out fishing, high winds overturned his boat throwing him into the sea. This angered Adapa who stopped the breeze that once cooled the lands.

Anu, the chief god, heard of the problem and wanted to know what happened. He discovered that Adapa had broken the wind and summoned Adapa to appear before him. Ea prepared Adapa on how to handle his appearance before Anu. He warned Adapa of the potential foul play he might encounter with the following words:

When thou standest before Anu
Food of death they will set before thee,
Eat not. Water of death they will set before thee,
Drink not. Garments they will set before thee,
Put them on. Oil they will set before thee, anoint thyself.
The counsel that I have given thee, forget not. The words
Which I have spoken, hold fast.
- Adapa and the Food of Life

Two messengers of Anu appeared and escorted Adapa on his ascension to heaven. Anu asked for his side of the story and Adapa explained what happened. For his honesty, it appears (there is damage to the original stone tablet) that Anu tries to offer Adapa a gift.

What can we do with him? Food of life
Bring him, that be man, eat."Food of life
They brought him, but he ate not. Water of life
They brought him, but he drank not. Garments
They brought him. He clothed himself. Oil
They brought him. He anointed himself.
Anu looked at him; he wondered at him.
" Come, Adapa, why hast thou not eaten, not drunken?
Now thou shalt not live." ... men ...Ea, my lord
Said: "Eat not, drink not."
Take him and bring him back to his earth.
- Adapa and the Food of Life

A similar prohibition to eating a certain kind of food comes to us directly from the Bible in the all too famous story of Adam and Eve. Not much after the creation of the world, according to the story, Adam and Eve are hanging out in the Garden of Eden. God told them they could eat fruit off any tree except for the fruit of the tree in the middle of the garden. God declared, "If you eat from that tree, heck, if you even touch that tree, you're gunna die". (OK, we took a little bit of creative license in representing God's words.)

Enter the snake. He tells Eve that God is lying. If she eats from the prohibited tree she would be God-like and know good from bad. Eve eats from the Tree of Knowledge and shares it with Adam. God figures the whole thing out and confronts Adam and Eve. Adam tries to blame the whole thing on Eve and Eve turns around and blames it on the snake. Everyone, Adam, Eve and the snake get into a lot of trouble.

God is concerned about Adam and Eve's bad behavior. He did not want them to eat from another special tree in the garden, the Tree of Life. Eating from The Tree of Life would bestow immortality on Adam and Eve, which would make them god-like. God, to avoid any further problems with the couple, kicked Adam and Eve out of the Garden of Eden. For their misdeeds, instead of the life of luxury they experienced in Eden, they had to start working for a living in order to survive. The fruit most often associated with this tale - the apple.

It is worthy to note that for something that we value so highly very little information comes to the present regarding specific legends associated with the miraculous properties of gold. Was amrita a form of gold that was ingested? It is possible, but the jury is still out. Regardless of what the precious commodity the gods were searching for in the milky ocean it has come down to us that the gods really did like gold and all things made of gold. Many texts describe the abodes of the gods as being decorated with gold. The gods are also described as adorning themselves with golden trinkets or riding in golden chariots.

Even the Bible discusses the god's desire for gold. Moses, after receiving the Ten Commandments, is instructed by God to build a sanctuary in which he would come and dwell among them. God then provides Moses with the instructions on how to build the Ark of the Covenant. He is also told of other objects God requires to accessorize the tabernacle including; a gold covered table for offerings of bread, gold lamps, as well as plates, bowls, and pitchers all made of pure gold.

The Aztec word "Teocuitlatl" provides us with another link connecting gold to the gods. Teocuitlatl translates as the "excrement of the gods" and is associated with their sun god Tonatiuh. The Inca describe gold as the "sweat of the sun" and associate it with Inti, their sun god. In Egypt, gold is thought to represent the "flesh of the gods" and their sun god Ra. Ra is depicted as a golden man. A similar tradition comes to us from India where Indra is described as being golden in color. Indra and the other Devas are also referred to as "the shining ones". The term the shining ones has also been applied to the gods of the Sumerian pantheon.

This universal concept of gold toned, shiny gods is a curious one. Were the gods actually golden in color? An interesting and solitary legend may provide insight into this enigma. It is the legend of El Dorado. El Dorado originally meant the "gilded person" or "golden one". The name, in later years, came to describe the lost fabled "City of Gold".

The real story of "El Dorado" is the tale of the ruler of the empire near Lake Guatavita in Columbia, South America. Each year, on the appointed day, the ruler would coat his body with a resin made of turpentine and then cover it with a fine layer of gold dust, thus gilding his body. He would then take a raft into the middle of the lake and make offerings of gold, emeralds and other precious things to the gods. His final act was to throw himself into the waters to bathe, washing the gold covering off himself, thus ending the ceremony and signaling the beginning of the day's festivities.

Another potential clue regarding the use of gold as a skin coating for the gods comes from ancient funerary rites. Masks, whether worn by the living or dead, played a role in magically

131

transforming an individual from a mortal state into that of the divine. Death masks, like the one worn by King Tutankhamen, allowed the deceased pharaoh to arrive safely in the afterworld and to gain acceptance as an immortal by the other gods. In Cambodia and Siam, gold masks were placed on the faces of their dead kings. The royalty of the Inca were also buried with golden masks. Did the gods cover their bodies with gold? Is that why gold was considered the flesh or sweat of the gods? If the gods appeared to us as being golden in color, could we in our endeavor to emulate the gods (and obtain immortality) have covered ourselves in gold as well?

Thus, the funerary mask moves a symbolic step beyond the ritual mask worn by the god impersonator in recording the final and complete transformation: the man has become a god. - Masks Of The Spirit: Image and Metaphor in Mesoamerica - Peter T. Markman & Roberta H. Markman

Why did the gods come here? We really still do not know. Their behavior, regardless of their true mission, is reminiscent of mafia kingpins, drug overlords or to be honest drug seeking junkies. Did the gods come here to supply their habit or did they discover an added benefit to life here on Earth? Could the precious amrita that the gods desperately churned for in the milky ocean be similar to the addictive mind expanding "Spice" as depicted in Frank Herbert's sci-fi thriller "*Dune*?"

One last point before we move on. We discovered something out of the ordinary in our endeavor to find references to gold in mythology or in the archeological record. While it may seem unrelated at first, we think you will find it as fascinating as we did. Gold mining, as some recent alternative history writers would like you to believe, was not the first kind of subterranean mining done on the Earth. If it was, we have yet to discover the location of the ancient mines that were used during the times of the gods. We also have yet to unearth the glistening fruits of their labors. The earliest objects made of gold were unearthed in 1972 in the Varna

Necropolis. The Varna Necropolis is located on the Black Sea in North-East Bulgaria. This site has yielded over 3000 pieces of finely worked gold jewelry buried with the grave goods. The site has been dated, based upon radiocarbon dating, to between 4600 and 4200 BC.

The intriguing point is this... When you delve into the history of mining on the Earth, what you find is not the prevalence of early gold mining around the world, but the mining of something else - ochre. Ochre, simply put, is produced when iron oxide (hematite) is extracted from the earth and crushed into a fine powder. It has been used for millennia as a pigment for paint, pottery and textiles. Ochre exhibits various colors ranging from red through purple, brown and orange to yellow, depending on its chemical composition. Historians believe that ochre was an ancient and universal symbol of blood, the liquid of life. What confounds both scientists and historians alike is that ochre, like gold, has no utilitarian purpose. So why go through the effort to dig up something that seems so unnecessary from deep within the Earth?

The oldest subterranean ochre mine discovered to date is the "Lion Cave" located in the Kingdom of Swaziland, South Africa. Scientists, based upon radiocarbon dating, feel secure in stating that this cave was first mined as early as 43,000 years ago! And they believe mining operations may have begun much earlier! Lion Cave is rich in ochre. Researchers believe that at least 100,000 tons of ochre have been removed from this one mine.

In Australia, stone tools were discovered on the site of one of Australia's largest iron ore sites. Iron ore is rich in iron oxide (ochre). The stone tools were found at the Hope Downs mine and are estimated to be at least 35,000 years old. In Peru, the Nazca people, made famous for the Nazca Lines, also mined ochre. They removed from one site, Mina Primavera, over 4,089 tons of material.

Ochre was used as part of the funerary ritual. Dr. Dennis O'Neil (O'Neil, 2011) informs us:

By 90,000 years ago, several Neanderthal cave sites provide the first reasonably good evidence of intentional burial of their dead. They presumably buried relatives and friends in shallow graves dug into the soft midden soil of their living areas at the mouths of caves and rock shelters. Usually the bodies were flexed in a fetal position. Frequently, the bones were stained with hematite, a rust-red iron ore. It is likely that the bodies were either sprinkled with hematite powder or the powdered pigment was mixed with a liquid medium, such as vegetable seed oil, and painted on the bodies. - Evolution Of Modern Humans: A Survey of the Biological and Cultural Evolution of Archaic and Modern Homosapiens - Dennis O'Neil

In Australia, at Lake Mungo, in Western New South Wales, excavated burial sites have yielded ochre-covered bones. Carbon dating of these bones indicates that these individuals lived approximately 62,000 years ago. Ochre, in addition to its use as part of the funerary ritual was used to cover the body of the living. It is still being used by many indigenous cultures as part of their ritual tradition. Maori woman are known to cover their bodies with ochre. We are told that they use it as a kind of insect repellant. Groups like the Himba people of South Africa are still using ochre. Women coat their bodies with a mixture of butterfat and ochre. It is seen as a symbol of beauty. The first Europeans upon reaching Newfoundland and encountering the native population observed that they covered themselves in red ochre. The Europeans referred to this group as the "Red Indians". Across the country in California, Native American tribes such as the Chumash were known to use red ochre as body paint as well.

Why was something like ochre so important to ancient populations around the world? The prevailing wisdom tells us that these cave dwelling, hunter-gatherers used it for painting cave walls and for ritualistic purposes. The bigger question is: Why would our ancestors start this practice in the first place?

Gary Gilligan, in his writing the *God King Scenario*, provides an interesting observation regarding the clothing worn by the ancient Egyptians. He notes that in every Egyptian relief, whether it is of a farmer in a field, a stone worker, a solder in battle and even the pharaoh, each person is illustrated wearing a loincloth while working out under the blistering sun. He notes that even today the intensity of the summer heat requires the population to cover their bodies from head to toe to protect themselves from being severely burnt in the scorching heat.

What is interesting when looking at these images is that all of the people depicted are painted orange or ochre in color even though pigment colors, including white, yellow and brown were available. Why were these individuals shown this way? Did they in life cover their bodies with ochre? Today, we still coat our bodies with fine particles of iron oxide. We use it to create a barrier between our skin and the sun's rays. We call this product sunscreen. Variations of this protective substance can be found in any drug or grocery store in the skin care aisle.

Did the gods, upon their arrival on the Earth also have to protect their skin from increased levels of ultraviolet radiation? Did they cover their bodies with a thin layer of powdered gold in order to protect their skins from the sun's harmful effects? Did our ancestors, in emulating the gods, choose to cover their bodies with ochre to look more god-like?

We would like to present a final piece of evidence associated with the use of iron oxide or ochre. Iron oxide formed early in the Earth's history due to the unique conditions which existed at that time. The early photosynthetic cyanobacteria (blue green algae) that came into existence when life first appeared on Earth released free oxygen into the atmosphere. Oxygen is a byproduct of photosynthesis. The free oxygen in the atmosphere mixed with iron particles that were dissolved in the seawaters that covered the Earth. Iron readily combines with oxygen when it comes in contact with water where it produces iron oxide. We recognize the byproduct of this chemical reaction as rust. Iron oxide, unlike free iron, is insoluble. Once formed, the iron oxide precipitates out of the water. In the case of our early Earth, it created thin layers of iron oxide on the primeval sea floor.

Oxygen levels did not build up in the Earth's atmosphere right away. It was about one billion years ago that the available iron became saturated and oxygen released during the process of photosynthesis remained free in the air. This change to the Earth's atmosphere is what ultimately allowed animal life to move out of the oceans and onto dry land.

Did you know that over the last fifteen years, unmanned probes to Mars have verified that the redness of Mars' surface is due to an abundance of iron oxide? Need I say more?

Conquest Planet Earth

Our narrative, Conquest Planet Earth deals with three specific themes. First and foremost is the battle that ensues between the gods for the ultimate control of the Earth. The second topic deals with accounts that describe the formation or reformation of the Earth proper. In some stories the Earth is created when dirt or mud is brought up from beneath the water that covered its surface. In others, land is fashioned from the body of a progenitor god. We will be discussing both versions. The last is stories that describe the placing of the sun, moon and stars in the sky. This vying for power and the formation and creation of the Earth marks of the end of the Second World and the beginning of the Third.

We left our story with the emergence of the coveted amrita from the depths of the Milky Ocean. The demon gods, the Asura, once the amrita appeared, rushed to seize it from the heavenly Devas. The Devas appealed to their supreme god Vishnu who transformed himself into a beautiful nymph. Her beauty took the Asuras aback. This clever diversion distracted the Asuras from their attempt to appropriate the amrita and granted the Devas the time they needed to steal the amrita-filled cup. (The Devas had never intended to share the amrita with the Asuras.)

The Deva Mohini, began to distribute the amrita to the gods. Rahu, one of the Asura, secretly transformed himself to look like a Deva and patiently waited to partake in its life-giving nectar. As Rahu began drinking the amrita some of the Devas recognized him. His cover was blown. To stop his ingestion of the amrita, Vishnu cut Rahu's head off with his discus. Needless to say, all hell broke loose. War between the demon sons of the Earth Mother Diti and the sons of the Heavenly Mother Aditi ensued.

And thus on the shores of the salt-water sea, commenced the dreadful battle of the gods and the Asuras. And sharp-pointed javelins and lances and various weapons by thousands began to be discharged on all sides. And mangled with the discus and wounded with swords, darts and maces, the Asuras in large numbers vomited blood and lay prostrate on the earth. Cut off from the trunks with sharp double-edged swords, heads adorned with bright gold, fell continually on the field of battle. Their bodies drenched in gore, the great Asuras lay dead everywhere. It seemed as if red-dyed mountain peaks lay scattered all around. And when the Sun rose in his splendour, thousands of warriors struck one another with weapons. And cries of distress were heard everywhere. The warriors fighting at a distance from one another brought one another down by sharp iron missiles, and those fighting at close quarters slew one another with blows of their fists. And the air was filled with shrieks of distress. Everywhere were heard the alarming sounds,--'cut', 'pierce', 'at them', 'hurl down', 'advance'.

And when the battle was raging fiercely, Nara and Narayana entered the field. And Narayana seeing the celestial bow in the hand of Nara, called to mind his own weapon, the Danava-destroying discus. And lo! the discus, Sudarsana, destroyer of enemies, like to Agni in effulgence and dreadful in battle, came from the sky as soon as thought of. And when it came, Narayana of fierce energy, possessing arms like the trunk of an elephant, hurled with great force that weapon of extraordinary lustre, effulgent as blazing fire, dreadful and capable of destroying hostile towns. And that discus blazing like the fire that consumeth all things at the end of Yuga, hurled with force from the hands of Narayana, and falling constantly everywhere, destroyed the Daityas and

138

the Danavas by thousands. Sometimes it blazed like fire and consumed them all; sometimes it struck them down as it coursed through the sky; and sometimes, falling on the earth, it drank their life-blood like a goblin. - The Mahabharata

The Asura, after a short time, realized that they could not compete with the deadly earthshaking weapons of the Devas. The remaining Asura, in an effort to escape, entered the bowels of the Earth, while others plunged into the salt-water seas. The Devas, now victorious, returned to their abodes in the heavens with the vessel of amrita in their possession and under their sole custody.

On eliminating the demonic sons of Diti and on acquiring kingdom of heaven, that eliminator of enemy cities, namely Indra, happily ruled the worlds... - The Ramayana

The conflicts between the Devas and the Asuras did not end there. The saga continues with Hiranyaksha and Hiranyakashyapu, two of Diti's demon sons. Hiranyaksha and Hiranyakashyapu, after having performed many religious practices had become limitless in power. Hiranyaksha with a desire for hegemony attacked the Devas. The Devas were defeated and Hiranyaksha drove them from their heavenly home. To prevent the Devas from regaining control, Hiranyaksha hid the Earth at the bottom of the ocean.

The Devas pleaded with Vishnu to save the world. In response to their prayers, Vishnu, in his third incarnation, assumed the form of the great boar Varaha. Varaha dove into the water and found the Earth at the bottom of the ocean. He used his tusks to dig it out. A battle between Hiranyaksha and Varaha the boar followed and lasted for a thousand years. Ultimately, Varaha was successful. He killed Hiranyaksha and brought the Earth back to its rightful place. The Earth could now be made ready to support life by shaping its surface.

Control over the heavens was returned to the Devas. At least for a short while. We will be returning to the ongoing battles between the Devas and Asuras shortly.

India is not the only country that has a rich tradition of the Earth being restored from underwater. The Iroquois Indians, from the northeastern United States, claim that once there was an island that floated in the sky. On this island lived the "Sky People". They existed before this world was created. According to their legends the Sky People lived quiet and happy lives. No one ever died and no one ever experienced sadness. One day, however, Atahensic (Sky Woman) realized she was pregnant and was going to give birth to twins. Her husband, in a rage, uprooted the tree that gave light to the entire island (the sun had yet to be created) leaving a big hole in the sky. The curious woman looked through the hole and could see the water that covered the Earth. In some versions of the story, her husband pushed Atahensic through the hole. In others, she threw herself.

Atahensic was very fortunate. During her descent she was aided by a fish hawk who used his feathers to pillow her fall. The fish hawk, realizing it would be unable to support her weight indefinitely, called for help in creating solid ground. A helldiver responded to the fish hawk's call and dove down to the sea bottom and brought up some mud in its beak. He placed the mud onto the back of a turtle and dove back down to get some more. Ducks joined in bringing up mud from the sea bottom. Some beavers helped to make the shell of the turtle bigger. They continued their work until the entire Earth had been formed. Atahensic stepped onto the dry land and sprinkled dust into the air. This dust created the stars. She went on to also create the sun and the moon.

Atahensic gave birth to her twin sons, Hahgwehdiyu and Hahgwehdaetgah. Hahgwehdiyu was the good son while Hahgwehdaetgah is described as being the evil one. Atahensic died in childbirth. Her body was used to fertilize the Earth. The two brothers, as time went on, fought a battle for control of the planet. Hahgwehdiyu, knowing his brother's evil ways, was able to defeat him with an enchanted arrow. The defeated Hahgwehdaetgah was banished to the underworld.

From Japan, we learn of the tale of the brother and sister pair of Izanagi and Izanami. Izanagi and Izanami were sent from the heavens to consolidate the Earth into dry land.

Hereupon all the Heavenly Deities commanded the two Deities His Augustness the Male-Who-Invites and Her Augustness the Female-Who-Invites, ordering them to "make, consolidate, and give birth to this drifting land." Granting to them an heavenly jewelled spear, they [thus] deigned to charge them. So the two Deities, standing upon the Floating Bridge of Heaven, pushed down the jewelled spear and stirred with it, whereupon, when they had stiffed the brine till it went curdle-curdle, and drew [the spear] up, the brine that dripped down from the end of the spear was piled up and became an island. This is the Island of Onogoro. – The Kojiki

Interestingly, as the story of Izanagi and Izanami continues, we learn that Izanami, like Atahensic also dies in childbirth.

In the Algonquian legend of Michabo, the Earth was once covered by a great flood. Michabo asked the raven to bring him a lump of clay, but the raven was unable to find any. He then asked an otter to dive deep into the waters that covered the Earth but the otter was also unsuccessful. Finally Michabo sent a muskrat into the watery deep who returned with some soil which Michabo used to recreate the Earth.

The Cherokee relate that at the time when the Earth was covered with water, all of the animals lived in Gälûñ'lätï, in a land beyond the arch. This land was very crowded and the animals desired more room. No one knew what was below the water when at last Dâyuni'sï, the water beetle, offered to go investigate. He traveled in every direction over the surface of the water. When no dry land was found, he dove to the bottom and brought up some soft mud, which began to grow until it became land. Once the

141

land had dried, the animals came down a rainbow and began living on the Earth.

The creator god Nzame, of the African Bantu tribe the Fans, created the universe and the Earth. Nzame decided that someone was needed to rule the Earth, so he fashioned the elephant, the leopard and the monkey and placed them in charge. Nzame was unhappy with his decision and decided to create something better. In his image, Fam was created. Fam was told to rule the Earth. It was not long before Fam grew arrogant and stopped worshipping Nzame. Angered, Nzame destroyed the Earth with thunder and lightning. Nzame decided to try again and renewed the Earth by placing a new layer of dirt upon it. Trees began to grow. Leaves that fell from the trees onto land became animals and those that fell into the water became fish.

The old parched earth still lies below this new one, and if one digs deep enough it can be found in the form of coal. - Bantu Creation Myth

In the Assyrian legend, the *Fight Between Bel and the Dragon*, we learn that Marduk (Enlil) was responsible for creating a place where the gods could dwell. He did this by laying a rush mat upon the water and placing earth upon it. Marduk, helped by the goddess Aruru, created the "seed of mankind", which included all of the mountains, rivers, trees, plants and animals that covered and inhabited the Earth.

We hear a similar tale from the Norse poem the *Voluspo*:

Then Bur's son lifted| the level land,
Mithgarth the mighty | there they made,
The sun from the south | warmed the stones of earth,
And green was the ground | and growing leeks."
– Voluspo, The Poetic Edda

Returning to the ongoing battle between the Devas and Asuras, Hiranyaksha is dead, killed by Varaha, the boar. His brother, Hiranyakashipu, is distraught by Hiranyaksha's untimely death. Hiranyakashipu blood boiled with hatred towards Vishnu. Hiranyakashipu began a practice of austerities and penance with a sinister plan in mind. He believed, as was tradition, that Brahma, the supreme god would reward him with mystical powers for the austerities he performed. His practice lasted for many years. With his newly obtained mystical powers, he planned on killing Vishnu and revenging his brother's death. Brahma was pleased by Hiranyakashipu's devotion. Appearing before him, Brahma asked Hiranyakashipu what he desired. Hiranyakashipu response was:

O my lord, O best of the givers of benediction, if you will kindly grant me the benediction I desire, please let me not meet death from any of the living entities created by you. Grant me that I not die within any residence or outside any residence, during the daytime or at night, nor on the ground or in the sky. Grant me that my death not be brought by any being other than those created by you, nor by any weapon, nor by any human being or animal. Grant me that I not meet death from any entity, living or nonliving. Grant me, further, that I not be killed by any demigod or demon or by any great snake from the lower planets. Since no one can kill you in the battlefield, you have no competitor. Therefore, grant me the benediction that I too may have no rival. Give me sole lordship over all the living entities and presiding deities, and give me all the glories obtained by that position. Furthermore, give me all the mystic powers attained by long austerities and the practice of yoga, for these cannot be lost at any time. - Srimad Bhagavatam

Hiranyakashipu, once he received Brahma's blessing, was virtually immortal. He began a reign of terror and dethroned Indra, the King of Heaven. Indra and the other Devas pray to Vishnu for deliverance. The Devas were told that in time Hiranyakashipu rule would come to an end.

143

Time passed and Hiranyakashipu has a son named Prahalad. Although Prahalad was born into a family of Asuras, he was a devotee of Lord Vishnu. Hiranyakashipu tried several times to kill his son each time to no avail. First he tried drowning him by tying a large stone to his body and throwing him in the river. The second time he tried to get Prahalad trampled by an elephant. Hiranyakashipu then built a house and put Prahalad into it and set it on fire. He even tried to poison Prahalad, but each time Prahalad was saved by Vishnu.

Finally, Hiranyakashipu, in a fit of rage once again threatened to kill his son. This time he challenged Vishnu to intervene. Hiranyakashipu, cursing Vishnu again, struck his fist into a column. The column split in two and the fourth incarnation of Vishnu, Narasimha, the half-man/half-lion emerged. Narasimha killed Hiranyakashipu with his claws in the threshold of his hall at twilight. Vishnu had calculated a way of getting rid of Hiranyakashipu by using Hiranyakashipu's own words against him. (See quote above.)

The final confrontation between the Devas and the Asuras ended with the fifth appearance of Vishnu in the form of the dwarf Vamana. After the death of Hiranyakashipu, Prahalad became king over the earthly kingdom. He had a son named Virochana and a grandson named Bali. Our narrative continues when Bali became the ruler of the Earth. Peace and prosperity were found everywhere under the rule of Bali. The Asuras, however, did not rule everything. The heavenly kingdom was still not under their dominion. It was decided that they would invade the heavens and take control of that as well.

Indra and the other Devas fought for many days against Bali and his armies. One by one they fled from the battlefield unable to face the strength of Bali's men. The Devas left the heavens and Bali was installed on the heavenly throne. Bali's reign was believed to begin a Golden Age.

In the mean time, the Asuras became drunk with power. They demanded the followers of Vishnu to worship them as the ruler of the three worlds. Indra's mother Aditi appealed to Vishnu

144

for the reinstatement of her son. Vishnu complied and emerged from Aditi's womb as the dwarf Vamana. Vishnu's appearance as Vamana the dwarf marks the end of the Satya Yuga (the First World according to the Hindu tradition). Based upon Five Worlds or Ages we are ascribing to in this narrative, this incident signifies the end of Second World and the beginning of the Third World.

When Vamana reached boyhood, he went to see Bali and begged for charity. Vamana requested a piece of land equal to three of his strides. Bali agreed to give Vamana what he wished. With his request granted, Vamana began to grow in size. He covered the entire Earth and the underworld in one-step and the heavens with his second. Bali, admitting defeat, offered his own head to Vamana, thus relinquishing the Asuras' control over the three worlds. The conquered Bali was banished to the underworld.

It is interesting to note that Vamana was the first avatar of Vishnu to appear in completely human, although dwarf, form. Each avatar that appears after Vamana also appears in human form.

Cronus, after re-imprisoning the Titans into the depths of Tarsus began his rule over the heavens and the Earth. Nevertheless, all was not well in Cronus' household. His parents, Gaia and Uranus, prophesied that one of his own sons would overthrow him, just as he had overthrown his own father.

Rhea bore Cronus six children, Hestia, Hades, Demeter, Poseidon, Hera and Zeus. When the first five of his children were born, Cronus swallowed them. Rhea, now pregnant with Zeus, approached Gaia and Uranus and asked them to help her devise a scheme to protect her unborn child. Gaia and Uranus sent Rhea to a place where she could hide from Cronus. When Rhea gave birth, her infant son Zeus was taken away and hidden in a cave. Rhea, upon returning home, presented Cronus a great stone wrapped in swaddling clothes. He took the infant in his hands and as he had done with his other children he thrust it into his belly.

Years pass without conflict. Zeus, now in manhood, returned to his rightful home and wanted to free his brothers and sisters from the belly of Cronos. In one account, he used an emetic (a substance to induce vomiting) which caused Cronus to regurgitate his children. Zeus, in another version, cuts Cronus' stomach open. This allowed his siblings to escape. Once released, Zeus called all the gods to Olympus.

The Olympian Lightener [Zeus] called all the deathless gods to great Olympos, and said that whosoever of the gods would fight with him against the Titenes, he would not cast him out from his rights, but each should have the office which he had before amongst the deathless gods; he said, too, that the god who under Kronos had gone without position or privilege should under him be raised to these, according to justice. - Theogony of Hesiod

Dissension broke out among the gods. Some wanted to get rid of the tyrannical Cronos from his seat of power, others did not want to see Zeus take command of the gods. Ultimately the gods chose sides and war broke out: Zeus and the Olympians on one side, Cronus and the Titans on the other. Not all of the Titans joined Cronos in this conflict. The gods who felt oppressed by Cronus' rule took up arms on the opposing side.

The battle lasted for ten years (a really long time) and no clear winner was in sight. Gaia, Zeus' grandmother, prophesied a victory for Zeus if he recruited the help of Cronus's brothers, the Giants, the Hecatonkheires and the Cyclops who were being held prisoner in Tartarus. He realized that they would be able to provide him with some powerful assistance and promptly freed them from their bonds. Zeus called for their help and they rallied behind him. The Cyclops, who were skilled smiths and adept in creating weapons, brought with them mighty weapons from the depths of the earth. They gave these weapons as gifts to the Olympian gods to thank them for their release from bondage. Zeus received thunder, lightning and thunderbolts, which he could use

146

to hurl at his enemies. Poseidon was given a trident, which could create mighty earthquakes that would swallow up and destroy their enemy. Hades received a helmet, which made the wearer invisible.

Armed with these weapons Zeus and the other Olympian gods overthrew the Titans and took control. Zeus, Hades and Poseidon cast lots for sovereignty. Zeus was given dominion over the sky, Poseidon the seas and Hades the underworld. The conquered Titans were bound in chains and sent to the cavernous gloom of Tartarus. The Hecatonkheires replaced the monstrous Campe as its guard. Cronus was also exiled to Tartarus, where he lived for 1,000 years before Zeus set him free. The control of the heavens and the Earth by Zeus and his cronies marked the end of the Second World and the beginning of the Third.

Another description of the war between the gods and demons comes to us from an unlikely source, the Bible. Many people believe that the prophetic Book of Revelation describes a battle between good and evil forces, God and Satan destined to occur at the end of time. Nevertheless, what if this assumption like many we have already visited, is wrong? What if the battle described is not of a future event, but instead is a recollection of the past. Is the battle between good and evil being retold as a warning of what may happen if we are not repentant in our ways?

(In keeping with the storyline we have been unfolding, parts of this narrative actually belongs in upcoming chapters. We have decided to include the full but abbreviated story told in the Book of Revelation here to reduce confusion.)

The Book of Revelation is a long and involved tale filled with angels and seals, plagues and heavenly beings, amazing beasts and details of the conflict between God and the inhabitants of the Earth. The highlight of the Book of Revelation describes the fall of the angels and features the heavenly war between Archangel Michael and the dragon. The dragon is often identified as the Devil or Satan.

According to biblical scholars, there are two groups of "fallen angels", the chained angels and the fallen angels. The chained angels were not cast out of heaven, but were instead sent into the pit of darkness, also called hell (Greek: Tartarus). Abaddon is identified, in the Book of Revelation, as the leader of the chained angels. He is described as having the body of a winged war-horse, the face of a human, and the poisonous curved tail of a scorpion. Hebrew writings indicate Abaddon and the other chained angels did not come from the heavens but instead from somewhere else. Where they came from is unknown.

The second group of fallen angels is defined as free angels in contrast to being chained. These angels are identified as Satan's minions who carry out his dirty work. Satan, according to some writers, was known as Lucifer before he was kicked out of heaven. The name Lucifer is translated as light-bearer, light-bringer or morning star. He is said to have been the leader of the Seraphim, an order of angels that surround the throne of God. In Hebrew, the word Seraphim translates as fiery serpent. The Seraphim are described as having six wings and are said to emanate a light so bright that even other divinities cannot gaze upon them.

To be honest, the Book of Revelation reads more like an all-out take-over of the Earth by God as opposed to a story of redemption. Briefly, God decides he wants to reign supreme over the Earth and demands submission over all of its inhabitants. Some comply with his demand but not all. The Earth is subjected to earthquakes and a number of violent acts. The residents of the Earth hide themselves underground in "*the dens and in the rocks of the mountains*". Many of the people change their tune and begin worshiping God after this first round of assaults. Another round of assaults strikes the Earth, again with mixed results.

God, still unhappy, opens the door to the bottomless pit and releases the demons that inhabited its depths. The demons are commanded to torment the inhabitants of the Earth for five months - that is, only the ones who had not surrendered to the will of God. The demons will be able to identify the uncooperative individuals because they will not have the seal of God on their foreheads.

The scene changes and we learn about a pregnant woman whose son is destined to rule all nations with a "**rod of iron**". Suddenly, a red dragon with seven heads, ten horns and seven crowns on his head appears. The dragon intends to eat the woman's child as soon as it is born. When the woman delivered her child, she flees into the woods to save his life. She escapes to a place that God has prepared for her.

The story then twists again and begins to describe a war in heaven between Michael and the dragon.

Now war arose in heaven, Michael and his angels fighting against the dragon; and the dragon and his angels fought, but they were defeated and there was no longer any place for them in heaven. And the great dragon was thrown down, that ancient serpent, who is called the Devil and Satan, the deceiver of the whole world – he was thrown down to the earth, and his angels were thrown down with him. - Revelations 12: 7 - 9

Casting out the Devil from the heavens marks the end of the current age. (What follows actually belongs in the next chapter(s) but is included here for consistency of the story line.)

The Book of Revelation goes on to describe the emergence of two beasts that were given the power to rule by the dragon. One rises out of the sea, the other the Earth. The inhabitants of Earth worship them. Their presence, however takes away from the absolute and complete sovereignty of God. I guess this irritates God because the next thing you know is that even more angels are seen flying around the heavens, tormenting the people of the Earth. That is, until we get to Revelation 14:14. John, the author of the Book of Revelation, goes on to describe a cloud he sees in the heavens. On the cloud is a man with a golden crown on his head and a sharp sickle in his hand.

Then another angel came out of the temple and called in a loud voice to him who was sitting on the cloud, "Take your sickle and reap, because the time to reap has come, for the harvest of the earth is ripe." So he who was seated on the cloud swung his sickle over the earth, and the earth was harvested. Another angel came out of the temple in heaven, and he too had a sharp sickle. Still another angel, who had charge of the fire, came from the altar and called in a loud voice to him who had the sharp sickle, "Take your sharp sickle and gather the clusters of grapes from the earth's vine, because its grapes are ripe. - Revelations 14: 15 - 18

The fighting continues and the Earth is scorched with a great heat and plagued by lightning, thunder and mighty earthquakes. It is also besieged by hail that came from heaven and with stones that were a talent in weight. (A talent is approximately 27 kilograms or 60 lbs in weight.) Finally, as we get to the end of the Book of Revelation John, the author, shares this with the reader:

*And I saw heaven opened, and behold a white horse; and he that sat upon him was called Faithful and True, and in righteousness he doth judge and make war. His eyes were as a flame of fire, and on his head were many crowns; and he had a name written, that no man knew, but he himself. And he was clothed with a vesture dipped in blood: and his name is called The Word of God. And the armies which were in heaven followed him upon white horses, clothed in fine linen, white and clean. And out of his mouth goeth a sharp sword, that with it he should smite the nations: **and he shall rule them with a rod of iron**: and he treadeth the winepress of the fierceness and wrath of Almighty God. - Revelations 19: 11 - 15*

In the end, the beast is vanquished and an angel comes down from heaven with a key to the bottomless pit. The angel cast the dragon into the bottomless pit and locks him up for 1,000 years.

While we have only provided a brief summary of its highlights, does it sound familiar to you? Hopefully, you were able to see the consistency of story line with the mythology of other cultures. We would like to suggest that you read it in its entirety. If read with this new found understanding of god, we think you will be as surprised as we were in what you find.

Then there is the little known story of the Jade Emperor and how he came to rule over the heavens. In the beginning, there were powerful evil demons who defied the rule of the immortal gods of heaven. The Jade Emperor wanted to help man cope with the harsh conditions on the Earth but he was just an ordinary immortal. He was discouraged by his lack of ability and limited powers. He decided to retreat to a mountain cave to meditate and expand his inner nature. The Jade Emperor during his retreat endured 3,200 trials, with each trial lasting for 3 million years.

One of the powerful demons who dwelled upon the Earth had ambitions to battle against the immortals of heaven and take control of the entire universe. He too, like the Jade Emperor, went into retreat to cultivate his inner nature. The demon passed 3,000 trials, which lasted 3 million years each. The demon, once he finished his final trial, felt confident he could no longer be defeated in battle. Power hungry he recruited an army of demons and planned an attack on the heavens. The immortals became aware of the demon's plans and prepared for war. Fighting began and the gods, led by the Three Pure Ones, were overpowered. They were unable to stop the demons.

The war was in full swing when the Jade Emperor finished his work and left the cave. His first act outside of his retreat was to cultivate the land so that it would be more pleasing to man. His work had not progressed very far when he saw an evil glow coming from the heavens and knew that something was wrong. Ascending to the heavens, he saw the gods in the midst of war. He realized that the gods were no match for the powerful evil demon. The Jade Emperor challenged the demon and a fight between the two quickly ensued. The mountains shook and the rivers and seas toppled. In the end, the Jade Emperor stood victorious. The other demons, who fought by the evil demon's side, were scattered over the face of the Earth by the remaining gods and immortals. The gods, the immortals and mankind proclaimed the Jade Emperor sovereign over all the land in return for his chivalrous deeds.

Scholars have theorized that the story we are about to unfold, as told in the *Enuma Elish*, the Sumerian god Enlil or Bel was the primary character and not the god Marduk. Marduk was the principle god of the Babylonians. It is believed that the Babylonians replaced Enlil's name with Marduck to elevate his status in their culture. The exact relationship between Enlil and Ea is not fully clear, but it is assumed that they were brothers. Regardless of their familial ties, there is strong evidence of an ongoing rivalry that existed between the two of them.

Ea, after securing his triumph over his father Apsu, establishes his dwelling in the watery deep in a place he called "Apsu" He is now in command of the council of gods. Some of the gods are upset by Ea's actions and do not like having him in charge. They approach the primordial god the Earth Mother Tiamat and complain.

To Tiamat, their mother, said:
"When they slew Apsu, your consort,
You did not aid him but remained still.
When he created the dread fourfold wind,
Your vitals were diluted and so we can have no rest.
Let Apsu, your consort, be in your mind
And Mummu, who has been vanquished! You are left alone!
– Enuma Elish

Tiamat agrees with the other gods. Something has to be done to stop Ea. Tiamat forms her own counsel of gods where they begin to develop a strategy for fighting Ea and the gods who are loyal to him. She elevates a god named Kingu to be the leader of her troops and commander of the assembly of gods. Her next move was to create monsters and weapons that can be used to attack Ea and his followers.

News leaks out and Ea finds out what Tiamat was planning. He goes to his grandfather Ashur and tells Ashur of Tiamat's treacherous plans against him. Ashur suggests to Ea that he talk to Tiamat and try to calm her down. Ashur reminds him that he had already killed Apsu and Mummu. Ashur then suggests that he kill the leader of Tiamat's army Kingu too. Ea approaches Tiamat but before he can face her he turns around and retreats. The gods under Ea's command are unsure of what to do. They elicit the other gods for suggestions. The god Marduk steps forward and volunteers to confront Tiamat. He only has one small stipulation...

He opened his mouth, saying unto me:
"If I indeed, as your avenger,
Am to vanquish Tiamat and save your lives,
Set up the Assembly, proclaim supreme my destiny!
– Enuma Elish

Desperate, the assembly of gods agree to his terms. If Marduk is successful in killing Tiamat he will have dominion over the entire universe. Making a very long story short, the gods provide Marduk mighty weapons including a bow, a mace and a net to use in his battle with Tiamat. Mounting his terrifying (their words, not mine) storm chariot, Marduk leaves in pursuit of Tiamat. Marduk calls her out on the evils she has conspired to commit and challenges her to one-on-one combat.

The fighting begins. Marduk quickly captures Tiamat in his outstretched net. Tiamat opens her mouth to consume Marduk, but before she can, he let loose the evil wind, which blows in her face and down into her belly. Her mouth held wide open, the winds fills her and her body becomes distended. Marduk then shoots her with an arrow that tears through her belly and splits her heart. Once subdued, he extinguishes her life.

With Tiamat out of the way, her followers tremble with fear, but they cannot escape. They are made captives, their weapons are smashed and they are imprisoned.

He made them captives and he smashed their weapons.
Thrown into the net, they found themselves ensnared;
Placed in cells, they were filled with wailing;
Bearing his wrath, they were held imprisoned.
And the eleven creatures which she had charged with awe,
The whole band of demons that marched on her right,
He cast into fetters, their hands he bound.
For all their resistance, he trampled them underfoot.
And Kingu, who had been made chief among them,
He bound and accounted him to Uggae (the God of Death).
                              – Enuma Elish

Victorious of his battle with Tiamat, Marduk creates the heavens and the Earth. He sets the sun, moon and stars into the sky. He establishes the days and nights and cycles of celestial time. He then decides to divide Tiamat's body up and do "useful things" with it. Accordingly, her body is split in half. Half of her body is used to establish the heavens. The other half is used to form the Earth, including its mountains and rivers.

A similar legend of the Earth's being formed from the body of one of the progenitor gods comes to us from the Aztec in Central Mexico. The four sons of the dual god, Ometecuhtli/Omecihuatl began their work creating the world. Their creations, as they labored, kept falling into the water, only to be eaten by the Earth Monster Cipactli. Cipactli is described as being a crocodile or the form of a half crocodile and half fish. Two of the gods, to save their creations, decided to destroy her.

One of the brothers, Tezcatlipoca, used his foot in an attempt to lure Cipactli to the surface of the water. His decoy worked but as Cipactli drew near, she bit off Tezcatlipoca's foot. In their struggle, Cipactli's lower jaw was injured leaving her too weak to

154

return under the water. Some stories say her jaw was ripped off. In both narratives Cipactli was destroyed.

Quetzalcoatl and Tezcatlipoca then formed the Earth on her back. Her hair was transformed into trees, flowers and grasses, her eyes became wells, fountains and little caverns. Her nose was changed into valleys and her shoulders were made into mountains.

In the Norse poem *Vafthruthnismol, The Ballad of Vafthruthnir*, we find a legend of the Earth being fashioned out of the giant Ymir's flesh. The progenitor god Ymir was the founder of the race of frost giants. Three sons of Bor, the gods Vili, Vé, and Odin, killed him. From his body they made the world. The Earth was fashioned from his flesh; his unbroken bones became mountains. His teeth were transformed into rocks and stones. Ymir's skull was then raised over the Earth to form the sky. A dwarf was placed at each of its four corners to hold it in place.

Pan Gu, who we met earlier, is the giant creator god of China. Legend states that after the death of Pan Gu, his body was transformed into the different features of the world. His arms and legs became the four directions and the mountains. His teeth and bones became valuable minerals and rocks that are found beneath the earth. His flesh became the fertile lands; his blood the rivers, and his sweat the rain and dew. His hair was transformed into the grass, and his veins became the roads and paths. His breath became the wind and cloud and his shout became the thunderbolt. His left eye became the sun and his right eye, the moon.

The African tribe the Boshongo relate that in the beginning there was only darkness, water, and the great god Bumba. One day, in pain from a stomach ache, Bumba vomited up the sun. The sun, now illuminating the sky dried some of the water, leaving dry land. But Bumba was still in pain and vomited the moon, the stars, and then some animals.

A traditional tale that comes to us from down-under involves the Rainbow Serpent. According to Aborigine legend, in the beginning the Earth was flat. As the Rainbow Serpent wound his

155

way across the land, his body created the mountains and troughs for the rivers. With the completion of the creation of the Earth, the Rainbow Serpent crawled into a waterhole to rest.

The Earth, according to another Aboriginal legend, was the home of supernatural beings. These beings were living beneath the crust of the Earth. With them were the embryonic or partially developed men. The tale tells us that time began when the beings came to the surface of the Earth. It was at that time that the sun and moon rose into the sky. The movement of the ancestors across the surface of the Earth created the mountains and its other physical features. The ancestors vanished back into the Earth when they had finished creating the world.

Pedro Sarmiento De Gamboa (Gamboa, 1907) tells us that after dry land appeared Viracocha was determined to create a new and more perfect race of people. He decided to create luminaries to provide them with light. Thus he ordered:

...that the sun, moon, and stars should come forth, and be set in the heavens to give light to the world, and it was so. - *History of the Incas* – Pedro Sarmiento De Gamboa

The Spanish friar, Cristobal de Molina, in 1573 reported that in a time, immediately after the deluge, the creator placed the luminaries in the sky. He goes on to state that the creator fashions a new race of men and woman. When they are completed, they were ordered to pass under the Earth and re-emerge in specified locations.

Thus they say that some came out of caves, others issued from hills, others from fountains, others from the trunks of trees. - Report of Cristobal de Molina

The account shared in the Book of Genesis sounds remarkably similar to what we have just shared regarding the beginning of the Third World. Genesis 1:9 - 13 (day three) tells of the gathering of water into one place and the appearance of dry land. Grasses, plants and trees appear next. It was only after the emergence of plant life that God places the sun, moon and stars into the sky. This occurred on the fourth day of creation (Genesis 1:14 - 19). Enigmatic as this portion of the Bible's creation story is, it is consistent with the mythology from other cultures.

Can we place a date when the war for control of the heavens and Earth took place? We think so. If we go back in time 432 million years (432,000,000), we find something very interesting. Four hundred thirty two million years ago places us right in the middle of the Silurian geologic period. A number of distinctive characteristics identify the Silurian period. They include a warm climate and elevated sea levels. A large portion of the Earth was covered by water. During this period, the first bony fish appear in the waters that cover the Earth.

Was life on Earth made in the image of the gods of the Second World, the half man, half fish beings who lived in the watery deep?

The next geological period, the Devonian Period, which started about 416 million years ago, surprisingly is known as the "Age Of Fish". Sea levels, during this age were high worldwide, and much of the land lay submerged under shallow seas. The end of the Devonian Period saw an increase in tectonic activity, which caused the formation of the mountains and valleys of the Earth. This period also saw the first seed-bearing plants and their spread across dry land. This, to us, sounded remarkably similar to the legends told of the Earth brought up from beneath the waters and tales of the mountains, trees, flowers and grasses formed from the body of a slain god.

The Devonian Period also saw the appearance of the first tetrapods (four-legged vertebrates) that began to move onto the face of the Earth. Could it be (as we stated in our exploration of the Biblical story of creation) that the placement of the sun, moon and the stars appears so late in the chronology of the world because life had yet to emerge onto the surface?

They say that history is written by the victor. Are the stories regarding the battles between the gods actually being told from the perspective of the gods of the heavens - the victors? Has our negative connotation of serpents, the devil and evil demons been passed on to us because they were the big losers in this cosmic battle? Were they really as evil as they have been portrayed? Is this why when we think of god, we look up to the heavens yet when we think of all things evil, we associate it with "down there"?

The question begs our attention: what would our world and our legacy be like, if the other guys had won the battle and gained or retained control over the heavens and the Earth?

The Rebellion

The Sky Gods were now in control of the heavens and the Earth. Myth, from what little survives from this period, states that the lesser gods were not happy with the new management. These are their stories.

Zeus, now victorious over the Titans, drove the Titans out of the heavens again and cast them into the depths of Tartarus. Gaia was incensed by the re-imprisonment of her children, this time by the Olympic gods. She rallied her other children, the giants, to rise up against the Olympic gods and reinstate the Titans to the throne.

The giants, a race of gods who sprung from the blood of the castrated progenitor god Uranus, were kept in subjugation upon the Earth. These Earth-born children wanted to end the reign of the Olympic gods and revolted against them. They disobeyed the rules that Zeus had set before them. They acted lawlessly and drove the cattle of the gods away. The giants, lead by Alcyoneus and Porphyrion, began a war against the gods of the heavens. The giants attacked the gods by hurling rocks at the sky and flaming oaks at the heavens.

Zeus, after his first battle with the giants, realized they were a formidable enemy. He knew he could not defeat the giants by himself and asked Hercules for help. The demigod Hercules was the son of Zeus and the mortal Alcmene. Hercules, responding to Zeus' request for help, shot an arrow dipped in the poisonous blood obtained from the multi-headed monster serpent, the Hydra, at the giant Alcyoneus. Alcyoneus fell but did not die. Alcyoneus was an immortal and could only be killed if he was outside his homeland, Pallene.

Athena, the Goddess of Wisdom and War, advised Hercules to drag Alcyoneus out of Pallene, thus leaving him susceptible to death. Once Hercules had Alcyoneus outside of Pallene, he beat him to death. He then turned his attention to the giants who had been wounded by the other Olympic gods and killed them all. The Olympic gods, with the help of the demigod Hercules, were able to quell the rebellion of the giants and confirm their sovereignty over the heavens and Earth.

At the conclusion of the battle, the bodies of the giants lay broken and beaten upon the land. Gaia, in order to preserve the memory of her lost sons, decided to create life from their remains. A new race of man was fashioned from the blood of the giants.

The fighting between the Olympic gods and the Titans was far from over. To fight the powerful Olympic gods, Gaia gave birth to her youngest and fiercest son, the monstrous giant Typhoeus. We will again return to the ongoing saga of the Greek gods as we continue.

From India, we learn of the story of Parashurama - Rama with the axe. Parashurama was the sixth incarnation of Vishnu. He, like Vamana the dwarf, appeared during the second age of the four fold Hindu yuga cycle. The Kshatriyas, the warrior and kingly class of the caste system, ruled the Earth during this time. The Kshatriyas were becoming arrogant in their powers. They believed they owned the Earth and that everyone else should be their servants. They oppressed their subjects instead of justly ruling them. The people started praying to Vishnu for deliverance. Their prayers were answered when Vishnu, in the form of Parashurama, was born. He was the youngest son of Jamadagni and his wife Renuka. Parashurama, after performing a great penance to the trident holding, serpent wearing Lord Shiva, obtained a divine axe as a weapon.

His father Jamadagni had possession of Indra's cow Kamadhenu. Kamadhenu had the ability to provide an endless quantity of milk. One day the thousand-armed king named

Kartaveerya visited Jamadagni. Mistakenly, Jamadagni told the king about his prized cow. The king realized that if he possessed the cow he could eliminate the problem of feeding his vast army. He also knew that Jamadagni would never part with it.

One day, Jamadagni left his home on an errand. Kartaveerya had his men sneak in, steal the cow, and take it to his kingdom. Jamadagni quickly discovered what had happened. The cowardly Kartaveerya, not wanting to be incriminated, killed Jamadagni. Parashurama, upon returning home was shocked to see his dead father. Using his yogic powers, he divined all that had transpired in his absence and decided to avenge his father's death. His first stop was to Kartaveerya, whom he killed along with his whole army. The rest of the Kshatriyas became fearful of Parashurama and sent their women and children into hiding. Parashurama, it is said, went around the world twenty-one times and killed all of the Kshatriyas that could be found.

Returning to the mythology from Sumer, we left off with Marduk (Enlil), after his battle with Tiamat, took control of the heavens and Earth. Marduk began assigning duties to the gods. He established daily tasks and the wages for this work. Ea encouraged the lesser gods, the Igigi to support Marduk in his new role. The Igigi ultimately bowed to Marduk's newfound power. While it is not directly said, it appears the Igigi were assigned the duties of performing arduous manual labors. Their labors are recorded in the Mesopotamian *Epic of Atrahasis*. The account opens with:

When the gods were man
they did forced labor, they bore drudgery.
Great indeed was the drudgery of the gods,
the forced labor was heavy, the misery too much:
the seven great Anunna-gods were burdening
the [lesser] Igigi-gods with forced labor.
- Epic of Atrahasis

The surface of the Earth, now formed, was dry. Marduk began a series of massive building projects. The Igigi, according to the texts, were burdened with digging watercourses, wells and springs. They heaped up the mountains and did other things. (The text is damaged here and we are uncertain of the full extent of their responsibilities.) The Igigi were also given the task of building Marduk's new luxurious home. Marduk's new home was intended to be a place where the gods could spend the night when they descended from the heavens for an assembly. It was to be built above the Apsu, the underwater home of Ea and was destined to be its Earth based counterpart.

The Igigi, after years and years of this backbreaking labor, began to complain. Their complaining turned into action and it was decided to remove Enlil (Marduk) from the throne. Rebellion was called and the Igigi set fire to their tools and their baskets. They then went out in the middle of the night and surrounded Enlil's home.

The anunna-gods, the Annunaki, tried to discover who had transgressed Enlil's command and instigated the hostilities. The Igigi gods declared they all had, and they listed their grievances. It was agreed by the council of gods that their labors were too hard. It was decided that they would create a primitive worker - man, to reduce their load.

Were the lesser gods pushed to the breaking point? Were their complaints justified? Is humanity, as we know it, the outcome of this conflict? The rebellion of the gods marks the end of the Third World and the beginning of the Fourth. Putting this narrative into some kind of historical perspective is impossible. Too little survives to place it into any kind of meaningful context. Some alternative historians conjecture that the period coincides with the Cretaceous–Tertiary extinction event, which put an end to the dinosaurs. This would fit nicely with our biblical timeline where we associated the end of the dinosaurs with the end of the fifth day.

The Age Of Man

We are all familiar with the first story in the Bible of creation. We explored it in detail in chapter two and concluded our discussion of the Book of Genesis, just prior to the creation of man. The first man and woman, according to chapter one of the Book of Genesis were created on the sixth day. They were formed in the likeness of God.

And God proceeded to create the man in his image, in God's image he created him; male and female he created them. - Genesis 1:27.

Many people are unaware that the authors of the Book of Genesis actually provide us with two different creation accounts. In chapter two of the Book of Genesis we return to the story of creation, but the narrative provided in this section is strikingly different. This version opens with a bare Earth. God proceeds to create a man, Adam, from the dust of the earth. He then blows the breath of life into Adam's nostrils and he becomes a living breathing soul.

God then makes a garden and fills it with trees to serve as food for his new creation. God puts Adam into his paradisiacal garden and assigns him the task of caring and cultivating it. Adam is told that he can eat from any tree in the garden, except from the Tree of the Knowledge of Good and Bad. God felt sorry for the Adam and decided to make him a helper to keep him company. From the earth, God created the beasts of the fields and the birds of the air. Adam was still lonely. God, trying to end Adam's suffering, caused a deep sleep to fall upon him and from one of his ribs God created a woman.

Biblical scholars, perplexed by the different narratives, have proposed a number of theories as to why the authors of Genesis would include two creation stories. One theory was the notion that God might have created multiple versions of man or humankind. Does mythology support this notion?

The *Popol Vuh*, the Quiché Mayan book of creation, discusses in detail the creation of man. The Earth, once the formation of its surface of was completed, was covered with trees and flowers. The gods decided that they should fashion guardians to watch over their creation. First, they formed animals, which they hoped would follow the commands of the gods. The gods wanted the animals to serve them by carrying heavy burdens. They thought that the animals would not resist their commands or contemplate rebellion. After their work was completed, the gods commanded the animals to say their names. They wanted the animals to know who created them. The gods, in return for their veneration, would help and support the animals. The animals did not speak when the gods commanded them. The animals, because they did not do as they were told, were punished.

The gods then decided to create a new race of beings. The new beings would have the ability to speak and would venerate them in the manor they desired. The gods, in addition to worshiping them, wanted these new beings to harvest the fruits of the Earth. The gods began to mold clay into a form they had imagined - man.

When he was complete they realized that this creature, unfortunately, would be of little value because he was just a lump of black clay, with a straight and stiff neck; a toothless mouth, wide and distorted; and blind eyes, faded and empty, placed without art or grace at different heights and at each side of the face, near the temples. Beside all this, they saw that this mannequin could not remain standing, because it crumbled and decomposed when doused by water. - Popol Vuh

The gods, realizing their mistake, set about making yet another version of man, this time comprised of wood. The new beings could walk upright, but their new creation seemed heartless and devoid of feelings. Its legs were not agile, it was not strong and it also had problems with its digestive tract. These new beings were extremely handicapped. The gods, frustrated with the outcome of their work, condemned their new creation to death and a rain of ash wiped them out of existence. The gods tried again and again to create the perfect being.

In yet another attempt, the gods decided to make four new beings, all male, out of ground white and yellow corn. Their bodies were reinforced with reeds, which added strength. They also created an elixir that would prolong their lives. These new beings, to the god's surprise, demonstrated intelligence and an understanding of the world around them.

The superior intellect and intuitiveness possessed by these men threatened the gods. It was decided to limit their faculties so they would only know what was revealed to them. The gods knew that in time the descendants of these first men would understand and perceive as much as their gods and creators. The gods, to keep the men from being lonely, created women. They were formed, as is recounted in the Biblical story of creation, while the men were sleeping.

The Sumerians and Babylonians were prolific when talking about the creation of man. Cuneiform tablets discussing the making of the first man include the *Epic of Athahasis*, the *Enuma Elish* and the tale of *Enki and Ninmah*. The description that follows is a summation of these stories.

The gods, after the rebellion of the Igigi, recognized the heavy burden, which they placed upon the lesser gods. The gods decide to create a primitive worker, a man, to bear the burden of the work. Ea was called upon to create this new being. Ea (Enki) took some clay from the top of the Apsu and he mixed it with the sacrificial blood of one of the gods. The god who was sacrificed was Kingu, who had been imprisoned after the battle between Marduk and Tiamat.

Numerous endeavors were made to create the perfect man. The goddess Ninmah made the first six attempts, each with poor results. The first man she fashioned could not bend his outstretched hands. The second man could not close his eyes. The third had broken feet. The fourth could not hold back its urine. The fifth was a woman who could not give birth. Although the text is damaged, we learn that Ea created the seventh version of man. He did this by putting semen into a woman's womb. Ultimately, the woman brought forth Umul. Umul was also afflicted with a number of physical disorders. In yet another trial, the god Nuntu mixed clay with the blood of the sacrificed god. She then had the Igigi spit upon the clay. It is uncertain what the exact combination finally created a fully functional man. The gods did eventually succeed in crafting a man who could perform the burdens of the Igigi. This new race of man is traditionally referred to in Sumerian texts as the "black-headed ones".

Figure 5: Tiki - The First Man

Tane, is a god of the Maories in New Zealand. He is the child of the progenitor gods of Rangi and Papa. He led his brothers and sisters in a rebellion that forced the separation of the heavens and the earth. Tane is identified as having created the trees and birds as well as the first man, "Tiki." (See figure 5.)

Padraic Column (Column, 1930) relates this tale about the creation of man. Aztec legend recounts how the Earth-mother, Citlalicue, gave birth to a flint knife. When the knife was flung down onto the Earth, it was transformed into sixteen hundred Earth-gods. (Is there connection between the flint knife, flung down by Citlalicue, and the sickle used by Cronus to castrate his father? Are the 1,600 Earth-gods the same as the Earth-born giants who sprang from the blood of the castrated Uranos when it hit the Earth?)

These newly formed Earth-gods lived as men and women and labored in search of food. After some time, the Earth-gods began to think that this work was below their station. They were, after all, the children of the Sky-father and Earth-mother. They asked their mother Citlalicue to make men who would serve them and bear the burdens they faced. Citlalicue explained to them what they needed to do to bring about this creation. The Earth-gods were told to send one of their people down to the place of no light, Mictlampa, and ask the Lord of the Underworld, Mictlantecutli, for a bone from the last race of men who had perished upon the Earth.

The Earth-gods sent Xolotl on this mission. Xolotl retrieved a bone from the underworld. Mictlantecutli, the God of the Underworld, gave Xolotl the following instructions on how to create a man from the bone of one of the giants who had dwelt upon the Earth.

This bone should be put into a vessel when it was brought into the Upperworld, and each of the Earth-gods was to put a drop of his blood into the vessel with the bone; out of what would brew in the vessel, two who would make the new race of men and women would come. - Orpheus, Myths of the World - Padraic Column

When Xolotl emerged from the underworld, the Earth-gods put the bone into a vessel and each of them added a drop of their blood. The Earth-gods watched over the vessel for four days when out of it emerged a human boy. The Earth-gods kept their vigil over the vessel and four more days passed when a human girl appeared. It is from these first humans that the current race of men and women are descended.

Hawaiian folklore tells us that in the first era, Kane dwelled alone in the darkness. In the second era, the gods Ku and Lono, along with Kane fashioned the Earth and all the things on it. The sun, moon and stars were then set into place between the heavens and the Earth. The third era saw the creation of man. Man was made in the image of Kane but by the hands of Ku. His head was formed out of white clay from the sea, his body from the earth and spittle. When the man's body was complete, Kane and Ku breathed into his nostrils and the man became a living being. By the fourth era, Kane who had lived on the Earth returned to the heavens.

The creation of man according to Chinese legend is associated with the goddess Nu Kua. The beautiful Chinese half woman, half dragon goddess Nu Kua emerged from the heavens to the Earth. The Earth had been formed from the body of the giant creator god Pan Gu. The Earth, upon Nu Kua's arrival, was filled with flowers and trees but there were no animals or humans upon it. Nu Kua felt lonely and decided to create animals to keep her company. Over the next six days, she made a variety of animals. On the seventh day, while sitting by a pool of water she grabbed a handful of earth and created a creature in her own image.

Nu Kua made scores of these new creatures. One by one, she breathed her divine breath into them and they came to life. Nu Kua got tired of the process of creating man, so she dipped a rope into the pool and pulled up more mud. She scattered small dots of mud upon the land, which became people. Accordingly, the people whom Nu Kua formed carefully became the rich and nobles. The beings who were formed from the scattered dots of mud became common man.

Did the gods create us? If we were fashioned by the gods, where did this take place? The abyss is where Sumerian tradition says it all transpired. Berosus, the Babylonian priest, according to Alexander Polyhistor, provides a description of the primeval abyss and the unnatural creatures that inhabited this underground realm.

There was a time in which there existed nothing but darkness and an abyss of waters, wherein resided most hideous beings, which were produced on a two-fold principle. There appeared men, some of whom were furnished with two wings, others with four, and with two faces. They had one body but two heads; the one that of a man, the other of a woman; and likewise in their several organs both male and female. Other human figures were to be seen with the legs and horns of goats; some had horses' feet; while others united the hind-quarters of a horse with the body of a man, resembling in shape the hippo-centaurs. Bulls likewise were bred there with the heads of men, and dogs with four told bodies, terminated in their extremities with the tails of fishes; horses also with the heads of dogs; men too and other animals, with the heads and bodies of horses and the tails of fishes. In short, there were creatures in which were combined the limbs of every species of animals. In addition to these, fishes, reptiles, serpents, with other monstrous animals, which assumed each other's shape and countenance. Of all which were preserved delineations in the temple of Belus at Babylon.

The person, who presided over them, was a woman named Omoroca; which in the Chaldæan language is Thalatth; in Greek Thalassa, the sea; but which might equally be interpreted the Moon. All things being in this situation, Belus came, and cut the woman asunder: and of one half of her he formed the earth, and of the other half the heavens; and at the same time destroyed the animals within her...But the animals, not being able to bear the prevalence of light, died. Belus upon this, seeing a vast space unoccupied, though by nature fruitful, commanded one of the gods to take off his head, and to mix the blood with the earth; and from thence to form other men and animals, which should be capable of bearing the air. - Ancient Fragments by I. P. Cory

Lewis Spence (Spence, 1914) recounts this legend shared by the Algonquian Indians of North America.

Then from the nethermost of the four caves of the world the seed of men and the creatures took form and grew; even as with eggs in warm places worms quickly form and appear, and, growing, soon burst their shells and there emerge, as may happen, birds, tadpoles, or serpents: so man and all creatures grew manifold and multiplied in many kinds. Thus did the lowermost world-cave become overfilled with living things, full of unfinished creatures, crawling like reptiles over one another in black darkness, thickly crowding together and treading one on another, one spitting on another and doing other indecency, in such manner that the murmurings and lamentations became loud, and many amidst the growing confusion sought to escape, growing wiser and more manlike.

Then Po-shai-an-kia, the foremost and the wisest of men, arising from the nethermost sea, came among men and the living things, and pitying them, obtained egress from that first world-cave through such a dark and narrow path that some seeing somewhat, crowding after, could not follow him, so eager mightily did they strive one with another. Alone then did Po-shai-an-kia come from one cave to another into this world, then island- like, lying amidst the world-waters, vast, wet, and unstable. He sought and found the Sun-

Father, and besought him to deliver the men and the creatures from that nethermost world. - The Myths of the North American Indians - Lewis Spence

A similar legend has been passed down by the Jicarilla Indians who live in the southwestern United States. This is their story of the creation and emergence of humankind. In the beginning, the Hactcin (the Jiarilla supernatural beings) made the Earth and the underworld beneath it. The Hactcin lived beneath the Earth in the unlit underworld. The most powerful Hactcin, the Black Hactcin, made the first animals out of clay. He knew the animal would be lonely so he made other animals from the body of the first. When he was done, he sent them to different places on the Earth to live. Some went to the mountains, others the plains, and yet others to the deserts. Next, he caught a drop of rain water in his hand and created the birds. Then he took some moss and created the fish, frogs and other water creatures. Feathers that fell off the birds and into the water became ducks and other waterfowl.

The animals knew that Black Hactcin was planning to leave. They asked him to create a companion for them in anticipation of his departure. Black Hactcin had the animals bring him all kinds of things from across the land. From the turquoise they brought he made veins, from the red ochre, blood. The coral became skin and the white rocks bones. Black Hactcin had created the first man. The animals were fearful that the man would become lonely. Black Hactcin had the animals bring him some lice, which he put into the man's hair. The man went to bed scratching his head and when he woke up there was a woman beside him.

The man, the woman and their children lived in the darkness of the underworld for many years. The animals were told one day to gather the food they ate. They mixed the collected food with a little sand and water and used it to grow a mountain. The mountain grew and the Hactcin and the animals climbed out of a hole that was in the sky that lead to the upper world. In this world, the sun was shining.

The new world was covered with water. The water was cleared away by the four winds and dams built by the beavers. The sun, instead of only shining on one side of the world as it had been, was made to go from east to west in order to light up the entire Earth. When the world was complete, the first people emerged from the lower world.

Thus the earth is our mother, and we climbed up as from a womb. - Mytha and Tales of the Jicarilla Indians - Morris Edward Opler

The Navaho and Hopi Indians of North America also have long-standing traditions of mankind's emergence from beneath the surface of the Earth. They state that there were four worlds, the surface of the Earth and three cave worlds, one below the other. Man, with the help of the gods moved up one level at a time until they emerged onto the surface of the Earth into the "glimmering world".

Parallel stories also come to us from the continent of Africa. The Bushman of Africa recount that at one time people lived beneath the Earth. They describe their subterranean home as being light even though there was not a sun. Here, no one ever wanted for anything and all of the people and animals lived together peacefully. When the world was complete, Kaang, their creator god, dug a hole all the way down to where the people and animals lived and helped them into the new wondrous world above.

Among the traditions of the Amazulu, a South African tribe, we learn:

We hear it said there are men in heaven and under the earth. But it is hard to understand what is the condition of these underground men; neither do we know what is the condition of those who are above. All we know is that it is said they are there. - The Religious System Of The Amazulu - Henry Callaway

It is said the black men came out first from the place whence all nations proceeded; but they did not come out with many things; but only with a few cattle and a little corn, and picks for digging with the arms... - The Religious System Of The Amazulu - Henry Callaway

Morimo, as well as man, with all the different species of animals, came out of a hole or cave in the Bakone country, to the north, where, say they, their footmarks are still to be seen in the indurate rock, which was at that time sand. - Missionary Labours And Scenes In Southern Africa - Robert Moffat

A subterranean abode for early man is also reflected in the Sumerian tale the *Creation of the Pickaxe*:

He created the pickaxe when daylight was shining forth,
He organized the tasks, the pickman's way of life;
Stretching out his arm straight toward the pickaxe and the basket,
Enlil sang the praises of his pickaxe.
He drove his pickaxe into the earth.
In the hole which he had made was humankind.
While the people of the land were breaking through the ground,
He eyed his black-headed ones in steadfast fashion.
- The Creation of The Pickaxe

Norse tradition informs us that after the Earth had been created, the Aesir god Odin created man. The first man was formed from an ash tree and was called Ask. The first woman was fashioned from an elm tree and called Embla. Odin breathed life into them. Villi provided them with intelligence and emotions and Ve gave them the ability to see and hear. Ask, Embla and the beginnings of the race of men dwelled in a fortress, which kept them safe from the evil giants. Its walls were crafted from the progenitor god Ymir's eyebrows. It is here in middle-earth, or Midgard, that man lived peacefully for many years.

Did the gods, once they created the perfect man, send him out from an underground world to live on the Earth's surface? Could the Garden of Eden actually be referring to this subterranean realm? Could stories of our emergence from the underworld be describing events similar to those experienced by Adam and Eve after they ate the forbidden fruit?

And Jehovah God went on to say: "Here the man has become like one of us in knowing good and bad, and now in order that he may not put his hand out and actually take [fruit] also from the tree of life and eat and live to time indefinite,—" With that Jehovah God put him out of the garden of Eden to cultivate the ground from which he had been taken. And so he drove the man out and posted at the east of the garden of Eden the cherubs and the flaming blade of a sword that was turning itself continually to guard the way to the tree of life. - Genesis 3:22 - 24

We wondered if it were possible to determine when man was created and emerged from this subterranean realm. We believe that myth provides us with some clues as to when the final act of the gods, the creation of man occurred. Even though there are only a few legends that can help us place the creation of modern man in historical time, when you listen to the stories the myths provide, and look for parallel details in the archeological record, a number of miraculous or at least very interesting coincidences present themselves; ones that we believe cannot be ignored.

We left our ongoing story with the rebellion of the giants and the battle that ensued between the giants and the Olympic gods. Gaia, at the conclusion of the conflict between these two warring groups decided to create man to preserve the memory of her lost sons. Greek legend tells us that the trickster god Prometheus was responsible for the formation of man. He used clay to mold his body and grass to cover his head. He then breathed life into his new creation. Prometheus became fond of man and wanted to make the lives of his new creations easier. Zeus did not want mankind to obtain any kind of power, especially the power over fire. Prometheus did not share Zeus' feelings. He stole fire and the crafts (the art of utilizing tools) from the gods, and gave them to humanity. For his transgressions, Prometheus was chained to a rock and was tormented day and night by an eagle who tore at his liver.

The appointed hour was approaching when man in his turn was to go forth into the light of day; and Prometheus, not knowing how he could devise his salvation, stole the mechanical arts of Hephaestus and Athena, and fire with them (they could neither have been acquired nor used without fire), and gave them to man ... And in this way man was supplied with the means of life. - Plato, Protagoras

We find comparable myths, especially ones describing mankind's acquisition of fire globally. In Hawaii, the trickster god Maui stole fire from the gods. He gave it as a gift to mankind. Native American traditions also attribute the attainment of fire to the gods. It was stolen from the gods and given to humanity as a gift. The culprit is often described as a trickster god who would take the form of a coyote. In Japan, the theft is accredited to a fox. Norse tradition tells us that it was Loki, yet another trickster god, who stole fire from the gods to aid mankind. It is interesting to note that mythology never tells us that man discovered how to make or tame fire. Instead, it consistently tells us that fire was given to humanity by the gods.

When did man first learn to use fire? Perhaps a better question to ask is what characteristics separated humanity from the rest of the animal world? We identify man from beast by a number of distinct features. These include our ability to walk upright, our use of tools, our ability to use and control fire, our ability to communicate with one another, and culture. One of the most obvious things that separate us from even our closest mammalian relative, the chimpanzee, is our apparent nakedness.

In the animal world, there is a limited number of hairless mammals. They are consolidated into two general categories: burrowing mammals and aquatic mammals. Species of burrowing mammals include the naked mole rat, the armadillo and the aardvark. The number of hairless animals increases when you include aquatic mammals such as whales, dolphins, manatees, pigs, hippopotamuses and elephants. The overwhelming majority of mammals that inhabit the surface of the Earth, whether they are scampering on the ground, climbing around in trees or flying through the air, all possess dense body hair. Man on the other hand is virtually naked. Except for the small amounts of hair on the top of our heads, in our armpits and around our genitals, our skins are completely exposed. According to Desmond Morris (Morris, 1967) *"If the hair has to go, then clearly there must be a powerful reason for abolishing it"*.

Most mammals have light skin. Their light skin is covered with a layer of thick hair or fur. Thick hair plays a vital role in the prevention of heat loss in cold environments. It also prevents the body from overheating and from damage due to exposure to the sun's ultraviolet radiation. These basic functions are critical to our long-term survival. Why would we, and not any other species of land dwelling mammal, have lost our hair? This question has plagued anthropologists for over one hundred years. In our search for answers, we discovered that theories abound.

Charles Darwin first proposed the thermoregulatory theory in 1871. It was supported by Dr. Peter Wheeler, a professor of evolutionary biology, in his 1984 work on the topic. The theory puts forward that early man lost his body hair in response to climatic changes. Three million years ago, the Earth entered a period of global cooling. The effect of these temperature changes on the environment meant that areas that were once forests transformed into dry grassland and savannahs. Darwin and Wheeler theorized that man lost his body hair when he moved from the trees to the grasslands. They believed that this change helped man regulate his body temperature in his new environment.

Others, such as Dr. Bernard Wood reasoned that it was the other way around. *"Bipedalism is a fundamental human characteristic,"* said Dr. Bernard Wood, a paleontologist at the University of Liverpool in England. He stated that our change in environment is what caused man to walk upright. Anthropologists agree that bipedalism, the ability to stand erect and walk on two legs, was one of the first major adaptations associated with our divergence from apes. Once upright, according to Wood, early humans lost their hair to help regulate their internal temperature. If we lost our hair because we could not stand the heat or if we walked upright first and then lost our body hair, no other animal on the planet has resorted to this approach to thermal regulation.

Dr. Mark Pagel of the University of Reading in England and Dr. Walter Bodmer of the John Radcliffe Hospital in Oxford proposed another theory. They suggest that man lost his hair in order to free himself from external parasites such as lice, fleas and ticks. This theory fails to explain why.

A final theory, but a theory that is often dismissed, is the Aquatic Ape Theory. Elaine Morgan, in her Aquatic Ape Theory, proposes that environments that give rise to hairless or naked animals are either subterranean ones (that is an interesting thought) and wet ones. The theory suggests that when our ancestors moved onto the grasslands and savannah they were already hairless or well on their way to losing all of their body hair. It goes on to propose that nakedness, bipedalism, and other modifications to the human structure evolved because we lived in a watery environment similar to the proboscis monkey from the mangrove swamps of Borneo, and the bonobo, or pigmy chimpanzee, of the Congo Basin. The largest obstacle the Aquatic Ape Theory has yet to overcome is when and where these changes occured. The fossil record is remarkably silent in this area.

As far as we are concerned, there is no big winner in the "how man lost his hair and began to walk upright" category.

Thankfully, there is a wealth of information regarding the evolution and development of man, forging a theory, stored in the fossil record. It is the dates, the timeline suggested by modern research that has held us spellbound.

Mary Leakey, in 1974, discovered a series of footprints near Laetoli, Tanzania. The footprints were made after a volcanic eruption in the area. The footprints were dated to have been created approximately 3.6 million years ago. The tracks belong to an Australopithecus Afarensis, an early hominid. A hominid is defined as a bipedal mammal, which includes both ancient and modern man. Australopithecus Afarensis began walking upright about 4.4 million years ago. These first hominids had not yet developed the large brain or skeletal features that identify a primate as a member of the genus Homo.

The impressions of the footprints are similar to those of modern men. The feet track side by side and do not show any sign of the creature's hands touching the ground. The toes of these human like footprints all line up strait and do not exhibit a toe that goes off to one side (divergent toe) as is seen in monkeys. They also show a well developed and permanent arch which is crucial for standing on two feet. The ankle bones of the Australopithecus Afarensis that have been discovered resemble those of the modern human. This indicates that these creatures were highly mobile.

The Australopithecus genus is not considered human. It is classified as being a hominid, but still falls short of "human". It was around 2.3 million years ago that a new creature appeared on the scene. Its name was Homo habilis. Homo habilis according to anthropologists qualifies as being an early human. It has a larger braincase than Australopithecus and shows evidence that some form of speech (communication) had developed. Homo habilis retained some ape-like features but was taller and had a smaller face and teeth than its predecessor. One of the most amazing things about Homo habilis is that this early form of man showed clear signs of using tools.

The first deliberately manufactured stone tools, called Oldowan, were made by striking off (removing) flakes from a pebble to create a serrated edge. They served as scrapers, choppers, pounders and even as a primitive knife. The pebbles, or cobbles, used were often composed of flint, jasper, obsidian or chalcedony. This technology was primitive. The importance of these simple stone tools is they provide the earliest evidence of cultural behavior. We had officially entered into the "stone age".

But it gets better from there...

It is with the appearance of Homo erectus that everything seemed to change. Homo erectus emerged in Africa around 1.8 million years ago. Its body and limbs were shaped much like our own. It also displayed a number of new traits that were not present earlier. They were identified by Harry Frankfurt of Princeton University:

- The brain size was increased over halibis ranging between 850 and 1100 cubic cm.
- Height also increased. Reaching close to 1.8 meters in male and 1.55 meters in females.
- The cranium is long and low and somewhat flattened at the front and back.
- The cranial bone is thicker than in earlier hominids.
- The face is short but wide and the nasal aperture projects forward, suggesting the first appearance of the typical human external nose with the nostrils facing downward.
- Pronounced brow ridges are present above the orbits.
- The postcranial skeleton is similar to that of modern man but it was robust and clearly heavily muscled.

In addition to these physical changes, Homo erectus lived a more complex life. By 1.5 million years ago, Homo erectus displayed clear signs of more diverse and sophisticated stone tools, which are classified as Acheulean tools. Acheulean tools are bifaced, which means that a cutting edge had been flaked from both sides of the stone. Homo erectus showed signs of cooperative behaviors. There is evidence suggesting they lived in small communities in a hunter/gatherer society and used oval-shaped huts as temporary shelter. Homo erectus also demonstrated an unmistakable ability to control fire. The earliest evidence of this skill has been found at Swartkrans, South Africa, which is about 20 miles from Johannesburg.

It was not long after the advent of Homo erectus that this genus moved out of Africa and traveled as far east as Asia. The cold climate of the new environment they inhabited also implies that they wore clothes to keep themselves warm.

"And Jehovah God proceeded to make long garments of skin for Adam and for his wife and to clothe them." - Genesis 3: 21

Returning full circle, one last item in our exploration into the creation of man is the question, when did we lose our hair? The first piece of evidence to support hair loss was the development of sweat glands. It is theorized that about 2.5 million years ago, hominids began to develop a great number of sweat glands throughout the body. Perspiring, or sweating, is the body's way of keeping us cool. It helps regulate our internal temperature. It is believed that sweat glands developed as a way to compensate for the loss of our insulating body hair.

Dr. Rogers, of the University of Utah, surmised that people would need to have dark skin to protect themselves against the harmful effects of sunlight once they started losing their fur. Dr. Rogers and his colleagues, Dr. David Iltis and Dr. Stephen Wooding, evaluated the melanocortin 1 receptor (MC1R receptor) for answers. The MC1R is a protein that is involved in the regulation of skin tone and hair color. Based upon the number of mutations to the MC1R gene found in Africa, it is believed that man achieved full hair loss **at least** 1.2 million years ago, but it is understood that this change more than likely occurred even farther back in time. Dr. Rogers also noted something else of interest when studying the MC1R gene. He found that all Africans have the same version of this gene, while chimpanzees, our closest living relative, expressed many different forms of it.

So far, we have addressed many of the characteristics that separate man from the animal world. We have direct evidence of our ability to walk upright. We have lost our body hair. We can make tools and control fire. We can communicate with one another and show signs of an early culture. What has baffled scientists is how in roughly a million years a species like Australopithecus who had a small brain, had a limited knowledge of tools, and was not particularly well adapted to its environment, evolved into a form with a much larger brain, could use tools and was well suited to its environment. Is it because we still have not found the missing link? Could it be that when the gods created man, the man they created was Homo erectus, or even the earlier Homo habilis?

Man, once created, took a massive leap forward with the emergence of Neanderthal Man. Neanderthals first appear in the fossil record around 400,000 years ago. The advanced stone tools manufactured by Neanderthals, called Mousterian tools, are marked by their increased complexity. Now, instead of tools being created for general purposes, they were developed to handle specific tasks. For the first time, stone tips were attached to spears. This allowed the Neanderthals to be more effective hunters.

Culturally, in excavations at Maastricht-Belvédère, "The Netherlands" reveal that by 200,000 years ago, Neanderthal Man had incorporated the use of red ochre into certain aspects of their lives. What they were using it for is still unclear. The discoveries in the Netherlands do show that the ochre was imported into the area, since iron oxide, red ochre, does not occur naturally in the local surroundings. This has led researchers to believe that red ochre played a significant role in life on Earth even at this early date.

By 90,000 years ago, there is reasonable evidence to suggest Neanderthal Man was intentionally burying their dead. The bodies in these early burials were usually flexed into a fetal position. The bones were stained with red ochre and in nearly half of the known sites; stone tools or animal bones were found in the grave with the bodies. In Shanidar Cave, in Northern Iraq, a number of burials were also found. The Shanidar Cave was occupied for about 30,000 years between 60 to 30,000 years ago. In one of these burials, evidence of medicinal plants were discovered. Soil samples taken near the burial site detected the presence of specific plant pollens, which included: yarrow, cornflower, bachelor's button, St. Barnaby's thistle, ragwort or groundsel, grape hyacinth, joint pine or woody horsetail and hollyhock. Each of these plants have a long history of possessing curative powers.

In recent years, testing of Neanderthal DNA has revealed something startling. DNA tests run on recovered 40,000 year old Neanderthal bones show mutations to the MC1R gene, the very same gene that produced dark skin in Homo erectus. The changes to the body caused by this mutation were expressed as the appearance of light skin and red hair. Scientists now agree, that at least some Neanderthals, instead of being dark skinned, may have actually had light colored skin, red hair and freckles, similar to what is seen in a segment of the population in the northern areas of Europe. Taken one step farther, researches have determined that people around the world, except for individuals from sub-Saharan Africa and Australia, all possess up to 4% Neanderthal DNA.

Homo sapiens, or modern man, first appear in the fossil record in sub-Saharan Africa around 500,000 years ago. This form of early man still possessed a number of archaic features. The discovery of Homo sapiens remains indicate that modern humans did not evolve from Neanderthals, as was once believed, but were contemporary with them. By 200,000 years ago, anatomically modern man began to appear. Anatomically modern humans, at this early date, lived exclusively in Africa, while the Neanderthals domain centered primarily in Europe. Asia at this time was still inhabited by the earlier Homo erectus.

The world changed again around 100,000 years ago when anatomically modern man began to move out of Africa into the far reaches of the planet. How our early ancestors traveled around the world is still hotly disputed. Finds in Israel, provide the first bit of evidence of movement out of the southern part of Africa. Skhul Cave, a burial site discovered in Israel, dates to around 100,000 years ago. It shows undisputed evidence of intentional human burial. The bodies found were covered with red ochre and a number of grave goods were present, including marine shells, which are believed to have been used as ornaments.

Stone tools, found in Yemen, a country located in the southern half of the Arabian Peninsula, have been dated back to around 80,000 years ago. It is believed that by 65,000 years ago this new form of hominid colonized Asia. Australia amazingly was settled a mere 5,000 years later. Researchers are still baffled as to how colonization of Australia occurred some 60,000 years ago. Australia was joined to Tasmania and New Guinea by a land bridge known as Sahul. Even at low sea levels, the Sahul was still separate from Southeast Asia. The only way to get to the Sahul, or Australia, was by some sea faring device such as a raft, boat or canoe. The movement of early man into Europe did not occur until much later. The earliest evidence of human populations in Europe was found in South-Central Europe and date back to about 48,000 years ago.

Genetic analysis of human populations from around the world has also revealed something remarkable. Geneticists, when comparing one geographical group to another have discovered that there are only slight variations between one population and another. They found that the largest levels of genetic variations occurred in Africa. This implies that these populations had a longer time to accumulate genetic diversity. This has also led researchers to conclude further that Homo sapiens first appeared in Africa. From their sub-Saharan location, a small group moved out of Africa and began populating the Middle East. It was from the descendents of this small group of explorers that the rest of the world was populated and settled.

The cultural and technological developments of our early ancestors and our closely related cousins the Neanderthals paralleled each other closely. By the Middle Stone Age, both groups developed the use of Mousterian tool technology. Both groups began hunting and gathering their foods. Both groups began burying their dead. Both groups started incorporating red ochre in their cultural practices. We were not so different from the Neanderthals as was once thought. Then about 40,000 years ago, something changed...

The Flood

The story of Noah and the ark is one of the best-known tales routinely retold from the Old Testament. The Earth, in God's opinion, was filled with debauchery. He decided to cleanse it by eliminating all of its inhabitants. One man, Noah, found favor in the eyes of God. God decided to spare Noah and his family from impending doom. To save him, God informed Noah that in seven days he was going to bring about a deluge of water and flood the Earth. He instructed Noah to build an ark and fill it with all of the animals that roamed the Earth. God provides Noah very specific instruction for the construction of the ark and the collection of the animals that were to be precluded from this disastrous event. Noah follows God's instructions and according to Genesis 7:11 - 12

In the six hundredth year of Noah's life, in the second month, on the seventeenth day of the month, on this day all the springs of the vast watery deep were broken open and the floodgates of the heavens were opened. And the downpour upon the earth went on for forty days and forty nights. - Genesis 7:11 - 12

The water that covered the Earth was so deep that it engulfed the tallest mountains. One hundred and fifty days pass before the water began to recede. By the tenth month, the tops of the mountains could be seen. All told, it took almost a full year for the floodwaters to drain from the face of the Earth and dry land to reappear. Why would God want to eliminate his creation? What lead to this decision? One of the most hotly debated sections of the Old Testament revolves around two lines of text that precede the story of Noah and are associated with the cause of the flood. The first, Genesis 6:1 - 2 tells us:

Now it came about that when men started to grow in numbers on the surface of the ground and daughters were born to them, then the sons of the [true] God began to notice the daughters of men, that they were good-looking; and they went taking wives for themselves, namely, all whom they chose. - Genesis 6:1 - 2

Genesis 6:4 goes on and informs us:

The Nephilim proved to be in the earth in those days, and also after that, when the sons of the [true] God continued to have relations with the daughters of men and they bore sons to them, they were the mighty ones who were of old, the men of fame. - Genesis 6:4

Let us take a moment and break down what these enigmatic lines are telling us. We know, according to myth, that the gods created man in his current form. Genesis goes on to tell us that the *"sons of the [true] God began to notice the daughters of men..."* One of the hallmarks of Christianity is the belief in one and only one God. If there is only one God, then who were the *"sons of the [true] God"*?

The Book of Genesis then mentions the Nephilim and goes on to relate that the sons of God had relations with the daughters of men and bore sons to them. Many people insist that the Nephilim were the offspring of the union between the sons of God and the daughters of men. The word Nephilim is often translated as "giants". The Septuagint; an ancient Greek translation of the Old Testament, literally signifies the concept of "Earth-born". Who were the Earth-born? As you may recall, from the Greek tradition, they were a race of giants who were created from the blood of the castrated Uranus that fell upon the Earth. It was this race of beings, who through their rebellion, called for the creation of man in the first place. Based upon our chronology, the Nephilim, the Earth-born, were alive and well and living on the Earth. If they already existed, how could they be the children of the sons of god and the daughters of man?

The offspring of the untoward union, when translated into English, tells us that they were "*the mighty ones who were of old, the men of fame*". In Hebrew the word used to describe these men is "gibborim". Gibborim is used to portray a man who is valiant, mighty, or of great stature. The Septuagint uses the term "renominati", which implies men of renown, men who have acquired a name for themselves through their exploits and enterprises. They were children of the gods, the heroes of old, the demi-gods, born part man, part god. Names of some of these men have come down to us through the ages and include Hercules, Achilles, Perseus, Hanuman and Gilgamesh.

Not all of the demi-gods were praised. Some were wicked in the eyes of God. They were corrupt. Violence filled the land. God, with sorrow in his heart and remorse for having created man in the first place, decided to eradicate him by flooding the Earth.

The apocryphal *Book of Enoch* also provides some insights into the misgivings of the gods and the reason for the flood. In addition to sleeping with the daughters of men, the two hundred sons of God (the Watchers) who were on the Earth taught humankind secrets, which were reserved for the gods in heaven. They taught humanity charms and enchantments, the cutting of roots, and the uses and properties of plants. They also taught humanity about the movement of the heavenly bodies and the constellation that filled the night sky. God, upset by the transgressions of his children, sent the angel Uriel to warn Noah that the Earth was about to be destroyed. In the mean time, he says to the angel Gabriel:

Proceed against the bastards and the reprobates, and against the children of fornication: and destroy [the children of fornication and] the children of the Watchers from amongst men [and cause them to go forth]: send them one against the other that they may destroy each other in battle: for length of days shall they not have...

And the earth shall be cleansed from all defilement, and from all sin, and from all punishment, and from all torment, and I will never again send (them) upon it from generation to generation and forever. - Book of Enoch

Azazel, the leader of the rebellious group, like the Greek god Prometheus, was bound and cast into darkness.

Typhoeus, the Titan storm god was the son of the Greek Earth Mother Gaia through her union with Tartarus. He is described as appearing like a man down to his thighs but with two coiled vipers in the place of his legs. Instead of fingers, he had hundreds of serpent heads on each hand and wings on his back. Typhoeus wanted to rule over the Earth and was well on his way to having both the gods and mortals on the Earth under his control.

Zeus, figuring out what Typhoeus was up to, took action against him. Seizing his weapons, thunder, lightning and the thunderbolt, Zeus struck Typhoeus with a preemptive strike. The Earth shook. Zeus poured fire from the heavens and burned the Earth. All of the heads on Typhoeus's hands were set ablaze. The mountains and forests were set on fire and the rivers and streams dried up. Between the thunder and flames created by Zeus and his blazing bolts of lightning, the ground, sea and sky boiled. Then with only a few stokes, Zeus crippled Typhoeus and cast him into Tartarus.

Typhoeus was hurled down, a maimed wreck, so that the huge earth groaned. And flame shot forth from the thunder-stricken lord in the dim rugged glens of the mount, when he was smitten. A great part of huge earth was scorched by the terrible vapour and melted as tin melts when heated by

men's art in channelled crucibles; or as iron, which is hardest of all things, is softened by glowing fire in mountain glens and melts in the divine earth through the strength of Hephaistos. Even so, then, the earth melted in the glow of the blazing fire [i.e. to form volcanoes]. And in the bitterness of his anger Zeus cast him into wide Tartaros. - Theogony of Hesiod

Zeus, after claiming his victory, took pity on the scorched Earth and wished to wash the fiery wounds from the land. Prometheus, the creator of man and the giver of fire, learned of Zeus' plan and warned his son Deucalion. Deucalion was known for his good deeds and his virtuous life. Though Prometheus was his father, Deucalion was a common man. Prometheus advised Deucalion to build a chest (a boat) in order to survive the flood. Zeus covered the entire sky with clouds and rain fell in torrents. The rivers and seas rose to cover the Earth killing everyone except Deucalion, his wife Pyrrha, their children and the animals that came to Deucalion to be saved. In one version of the story, individuals who had escaped to high mountain peaks also survived.

A similar narrative comes to us from the *Epic of Gilgamesh*, the earliest surviving work of Mesopotamian literature. Gilgamesh, in an effort to achieve immortality, goes in search of Utnapishtim, the survivor of the great flood in the depths of the underworld. Utnapishtim was granted immortality by the gods. Gilgamesh, upon meeting Utnapishtim, learns the details of the deluge.

Utnapishtim spoke to Gilgamesh, saying: "I will reveal to you, Gilgamesh, a thing that is hidden, a secret of the gods I will tell you!" - Epic of Gilgamesh

At a time before the flood the people of the Earth multiplied. Their noise and constant clamor disturbed the gods, especially Enlil. Enlil complained to the counsel of gods about the noise and the gods were moved by his words. It was decided to let loose a deluge to eliminate mankind. All of the gods in the counsel (Anu, Enlil, Ninurta, Ennugi and Ea) took an oath of secrecy to keep their plan quiet from mankind and the other gods. Ea, keeping his word of non-disclosure, instead of repeating the intentions of the gods to mortal man, spoke them to a reed house, the reed house inhabited by Utnapishtim.

> *Reed house, reed house! Wall, wall!*
> *O man of Shuruppak, son of Ubartutu:*
> *Tear down the house and build a boat!*
> - Epic of Gilgamesh

Utnapishtim, like Noah, was provided with specific instructions for building a craft. The plans called for the construction of six decks and seven levels and were designed to keep water out. The craft was loaded with all of the beast and animals of the field, Utnapishtim's family and the craftsmen who helped build the boat.

The sky turned black and the storm began. The dikes overflowed with water and by day's end the mountains were submerged. The gods were frightened by the flood. Some of the gods escaped by ascending into the heaven of Anu. The gods who were not saved crouched cowering by the outer wall of the city of Shuruppak. The surviving gods wept as they watched many of the gods, their creation and mankind being destroyed.

The storms raged for seven days. According to Utnapishtim, *"the terrain was as flat as a roof"*. He searched in every direction for dry land and in the distance he saw the peak of Mount Nimush, upon which he moored his craft. On the seventh day, after the rains had subsided, Utnapishtim released a dove, which circled and came back. He then let a swallow loose, only to have it return. Finally a raven was sent off which did not come back.

In the Sumerian *Epic of Atrahasis* we find a related tale except in this version the actions of the gods are much more sinister. We learn that 1,200 years after the creation of mankind the number of people who inhabited the Earth had grown. Their

190

noise and ruckus started disturbing Enlil's sleep. Enlil decided to let lose a plague in order to reduce the surplus population. This seemed to work for a while. Another 1,200 years passed and again Enlil is bothered by the noise. This time, in order to reduce their numbers, he has the Thunder-rain god Adad hold back the rains and the world suffers from a great drought.

The rains eventually returned and another 1,200 years go by. The population continues to grow, but this time the noise becomes too much for Enlil to bear. Hoping to alleviate his problem he tells the gods to hold back all of nature's gifts. This went on for six years and as the texts describes, the people of Earth were reduced to cannibalism in order to survive. Enki tried to save the people from starvation. This angered Enlil even more. Enlil decided to take out mankind once and for all. He planned to do this by flooding the world.

Cultures around the Mediterranean Sea are not the only societies who have stories of a catastrophic flood. Juan Polo de Ondegardo (a Spanish chronicler) writing in the mid 1500's was shocked when he learned of the Incan story of the deluge. "...*how is it possible that these Indians can have had any knowledge of the deluge?*" he asks. This is the story, shared by the Inca, about the devastating flood that decimated their populations.

In the highlands of Peru there were two brothers who were above reproach. They lived during a time called Pachachama, a period when humanity did whatever it pleased. The people during this time were cruel and barbaric, planning wars and ignoring the precepts of the gods. One day the two shepherd brothers noticed their llamas acting peculiarly. The brothers asked the llamas what was going on. The llamas warned the brothers that a great flood was coming that would destroy all of the creatures on the Earth. Seeking safety, the brothers took their families and animals and climbed the highest mountain and sought shelter in its caves.

The rain began to fall and continued relentlessly for months. The mountain, as the waters continued rising, grew taller and taller. When the rain stopped and the waters subsided, the mountain returned to its original height. The brothers and their families left the caves and repopulated the earth.

We find a remarkably similar story from Australia. Mungan Ngour, the Father God of the Kurnai Koori people of Victoria Australia put his son Tundun in charge of the rules and secret ceremonies for initiation of boys into manhood. Somehow, the woman of the tribe discovered their secrets and Mungan Ngour became angry. People began to run amok, killing one another. Chaos ensued. Finally, the seas rushed in and flooded the land. Mungan Ngour ascended into the sky. This ended the Altjeringa or Dream Time of the aboriginal people.

Hans Schindler Bellamy in his 1936 book *Moons, Myths and Men,* estimates that there are over 500 Flood legends worldwide. Without recounting each of these legends, we find that the level of corroboration between the myths is impeccable. Differences between the flood myths of each culture are not found in pockets or regions of the world but are evenly distributed around the globe including: North America, South America, Africa, India, China, Australia, the Middle East and Europe.

The reason given for the flood, in many myths, was that the gods were displeased with mankind or that the people didn't follow the laws ordained by the gods. In the majority of the stories, certain individuals are warned of the impending disaster. They are often described as being righteous, virtuous or pious. The method of escaping the raging waters ranges from a boat, a raft, a canoe, a log, a reed, a box or a leaf. Individuals, in some accounts, survive by climbing a high mountain or tall tree. The survivors are often depicted as a husband and wife pair (and their children) or as brother and sister. Many accounts also include animals as having survived the pandemic. A number of cultures also recount a bird or other animal being sent out to find dry land before the boat is disembarked.

Putting the flood into some historical context is challenging. Biblical historians believe that the flood occurred around 2400 BCE. Others contend that it happened about 6,000 years ago, just prior to the advent of civilization.

Current research into the Earth's past place the flood around 11,000 years ago at the end of the "last ice age". The last ice age began approximately 110,000 years ago and peaked (was at its glacial maximum) 20,000 years ago. During this extended period of reduced global temperatures, water was taken from the Earth's oceans and formed ice sheets. Global sea levels dropped by about 110 meters. This exposed the continental shelves and land bridges such as the one that extends between the Soviet Union and Alaska.

The enormous ice sheets began to melt as temperatures rose, releasing massive amounts of water. Sea levels started rising. It is estimated that the average rate of runoff water from the melting ice sheets that returned to the ocean was 1 to 2.5 meters per century. The total rise in sea level, by the time the last ice age ended, was 120 meters. This slow and gradual increase in sea levels, in our humble opinion, can hardly explain the stories of a massive flood that devastated mankind.

Evidence of a major geological event that could have resulted in a global flood does exist during this period of time but is unsubstantiated and is often dismissed. About 12,900 years ago, as global temperatures were increasing, the world saw a brief but rapid return to glacial conditions. This interglacial period was termed the Younger Dryas.

Researchers believe that the increase in melting glacial waters caused changes to the oceans currents. These changes set off another quick and deep freeze. The Younger Dryas lasted for about 1,400 years, and ended 11,500 years ago. During this time, temperatures in Europe are estimated to have dropped about 7° in only 20 years. Investigators studying animals, such as mammoths found frozen in Siberia, look to this event as a possible explanation as to why these animals appeared to have been flash frozen in place.

Associated with the timing of the Younger Dryas is a thin layer of sedimentary material that dates back to about 12,900 years ago. This layer of sedimentation contains magnetic grains, microspherules containing iridium (iridium is an element not native to the Earth that can be found in the layer of sedimentation that separates the age of dinosaurs from the next epoch. It is found in the KT boundary), glass-like carbon, charcoal and soot. This date also corresponds to the demise of the Clovis culture of North America and the Magdalenian culture in Europe. It is also analogous to dates associated with the Holocene extinction where a large number of plants and animals, including the megafauna, died.

It is believed by some that the Younger Dryas was triggered by an extraterrestrial (meteor) impact that destabilized glacial ice sheets and caused changes to the Earth's ocean's circulation. James Maruske, a Nuclear Physicist and expert in comet/asteroid impacts has suggested that the impact of a comet could well explain the narratives described in flood accounts. Heat and energy that is released as a result of the initial impact could produce a partial glacial ice melt. Water runoff from the destabilized ice and the movement of glacial masses into the oceans could cause an immediate rise in sea levels. Super heated steam would also be produced, which would rise into the atmosphere and fall back to the Earth in the form of violent storms. Theoretically speaking, heavy rain could be experienced for several days if not weeks. Maruske believed that sea levels could rise as much as 400 feet, submerging approximately 15 million square miles of coastline around the world.

The extraterrestrial impact that may have precipitated the Younger Dryas boundary is thought by some to have struck the southeastern coast of the United States and formed the Carolina Bays. The concept of an extraterrestrial impact as the cause for the formation of the Carolina Bays is still being argued in scientific circles.

This is where we ran into some problems. Even with the information we have just provided, there is still not any hard core, smoking gun evidence of a global flood. When we looked at the mythical and historical record of our ancestors, we discover something significantly different. The authors, who do provide dates for the flood, place this global catastrophe at a time that far exceeds the dates proposed by scientists. The clearest and most direct record we have regarding the flood from antiquity comes from the Sumerian Kings List.

The Sumerian Kings List is an ancient cuneiform document that lists the names of each king of Sumner and the length of their rule. Scholars dismiss the extended length of reign ascribed to each king. Here, we say again, could the scholars be wrong?

In 5 cities 8 kings; they ruled for 241,200 years.
Then the flood swept over.
After the flood had swept over, and the kingship had descended
from heaven, the kingship was in Kic.
-Sumerian King List

Based upon historical Sumerian and Babylonian documents we know that King Ur-Nungal (Ur-Nammu), lived between 2113 and 2095 BCE. His name is also memorialized on the Sumerian Kings List as being the son of Gilgamesh. Starting with Ur-Nungal and counting back the length of rule of each of the preceding kings back to the time of the flood we arrive at a date around 30,000 BCE or about 32,000 years ago. Berosus, the Babylonian priest, in his writings places the date of the flood circa 39,000 years ago.

These dates, while seeming outlandish, are supported by parallel dates for some undisclosed "recorded event" worldwide. In China, *The Records of the Grand Historian* by Sima Qian states that there were three sovereigns (Three August Ones) who were demigods or god-kings. The first was Fu Xi who ruled for 18,000 years. The next was Nüwa who ruled for 11,000 years and then finally Shennong, who is often identfied with the Yellow Emperor. According to legends from China, Fu Xi and Nüwa his sister were the only ones who survived when a great flood swept over the land. 18,000 + 11,000 + 5,600 = 34,600 years ago. Manetho, the ancient Egyptian historian, describes a period of time some 35,000 years ago as when the gods ruled the Earth.

The Dresden Codex, a pre-Columbian Mayan manuscript written in the eleventh or twelfth century, is one of four authentic Mayan books that have survived into the current era. It contains astronomical tables for the movement of planets, which are so accurate that it astounds modern astronomers. On pages 61 - 69 of this incredible text are references to dates which go back about 34,000 years. Unfortunately, the text fails to describe what occurred on these dates.

When we looked at the geological record, we are not able to find evidence to support a global flood 34,000 years ago. Is it because it did not happen circa 34,000 BCE? Another possibility, as to why there is no record of a flood 34,000 years ago, is that no one has ever looked for evidence of a global calamity that far back in time.

Hard geological facts have yet to surface to provide us with a conclusive date for the flood. Perhaps some clues can be found by looking at our continuing evolution. A surprising number of correlations seem to emerge when we evaluated a timeline for the development of the culture and implements used by anatomically modern man.

Starting with a date of around 40,000 years ago and moving forward, we find three major radar-like blips on the currently accepted timeline of human advancement. The first blip occurred some 30 - 40,000 years ago which seemly coincides with the date of the flood that is recorded in our written and mythological history. The second occurs about 11,500 years ago with the currently accepted date of the flood. The third date parallels the rise of civilization and has been dated as having occurred some 5 - 6,000 years ago.

Scientists agree at about 40,000 years ago the Neanderthals were quickly heading for extinction. How or why this occurred is speculative at best. Could the flood described in these ancient records be describing a time when the gods "cleansed the earth" -- of Neanderthals? Could the descent of kingship from the heavens (500,000 - 271,000 years ago), as stated by Berosus and the Sumerian Kings List, document a time when the demigods, the offspring of the sons of god and the daughters of man, began populating the Earth? Did the flood get rid of these abominations as well as the remaining giants? Then, when the flood had subsided, humanity, as we know it, was the dominant intelligent species left on the planet.

From the archeological record, we do know that around 35,000 years ago, mankind made huge strides in culture and technology. He began to express himself in a completely new way. These changes were a clear departure from all other earlier behaviors. It is called, in some circles, the "creative explosion". It is represented by man's ability to utilize symbolic thought to create and represent things in his environment.

The creative explosion saw the rise of the first intricate cave paintings, such as the ones found in Chauvet in France which included representations of animals such as bison, horses, aurochs, and deer. Man started recording information, such as numbers, quantities and even messages, on pieces of bone, ivory, wood or stone on what are called tally sticks. Advances in weaponry brought about the emergence of the atlatl, a spear thrower that allowed our ancestors to hurl a dart up to 40 meters.

Evidence of cut, twisted and dyed flax fibers have been discovered in the Dzudzuana Cave, in the Republic of Georgia, which suggests that the early stages of weaving and textile production may have begun. The donning of clothing, through the use of sewing was soon to follow. The first figurative piece of art, as opposed to abstract designs, called the Venus of Schelklingen (Venus of Hohle Fels), was unearthed near Schelklingen Germany. Pottery, the molding and firing of clay, made its debut where it was fashioned into Venus or Grimaldi figurines.

Man also started collecting and grinding wild cereal grains, wheat and barley, and began baking bread. For people around the world, bread wheat (Triticum aestivum) is now a food staple. Bread wheat came into existence because of two rare genetic events, both of which happened during the Stone Age, in the region of the Middle East known as the Fertile Crescent. Typically, different genetic species cannot interbreed and produce a viable hybrid offspring. The first genetic interbreeding anomaly happened about 30,000 years ago when a wild einkorn wheat (Triticum monococcum) mixed with a species of goat grass (Aegilops speltoides) and produced a primitive wheat known as emmer wheat.

Emmer wheat has a higher quantity gluten as opposed to einkorn wheat. Gluten is what holds a loaf of bread together. It is the elastic nature of gluten that allows dough to rise in the oven and produce the lighter texture we associate with wheat bread.

Between 25 and 15,000 years ago, weaponry again took another major leap forward with the invention of the bow and arrow. In the arts, Venus figures were frequently depicted as wearing clothes. Pottery, in the form of pots and other utilitarian items, appear in the Hunan province of southern China and in Japan during the Jomon period. The rudiments of culture, while in its infancy in the past, appeared fully grown. Many of the things we see in society today, such as music, art and religious expression, were now in place.

Then, for some reason, things quiet down and our fast forward motion slowed to a crawl...

The domestication of plants and animals put us back on the fast track. This took place around 10,000 years ago. The dog, by this point in our history, had long been domesticated. The first plant species to be domesticated was the bottle gourd. Bottle gourds served as containers before the invention of clay or stone pottery. They were first domesticated in Asia approximately 10,000 years ago, if not earlier. The use of the domestic bottle gourd for utilitarian purposes quickly found its way into North America. (The bottle gourd was the first domesticated plant species. This fact is frequently overlooked by historians placing the origin of domesticated plants and the birth of agriculture in the Fertile Crescent.)

Genetic analysis of the earliest cultivated form of wheat suggests that wild einkorn wheat was first grown in the upper fringe of the Fertile Crescent, in the Karacadag Mountains in southeastern Turkey. The Karacadag Mountains are only about 30 km from the now famous prehistoric site of Göbekli Tepe. The main difference between wild wheat and domesticated wheat is that domesticated wheat has larger seeds and a non-shattering rachis. The rachis is what holds a grain of wheat to the plant stem. In wild grains, the rachis is brittle which allows for the easy dissemination of the plant seeds. The natural seed dispersal of a plant with a non-shattering rachis is eliminated or greatly reduced, thus increasing crop yield.

Evidence suggests that it only took two to three centuries for early farmers to domesticate wheat, sometime between 10,000 and 9700 BCE. Scientists are hard-pressed to envision how such a large number of physiological changes between their wild progenitors and even the most primitive forms of wheat could take place naturally in such a short time. In light of this evidence, they believe that some sort of artificial selection was used to accelerate its transformation.

At about the same time, the second of the aforementioned rare genetic events that affected wheat took place. This time the newly emerged emmer wheat somehow interbred with a different species of wild goat grass. The net result of this mix produced a wheat hybrid whose seeds were even larger than in the past. This new form of wheat became a popular breed for early farmers. Descendents of this new species of wheat are still being farmed today.

With the emergence of the first domesticated plants, it seems the concept of domestication caught on like wildfire. Early domestic forms of plants, such as fig trees, rice, chickpeas, potatoes, beans, squash, maize, millet, avocados, cotton and bananas quickly followed. One would logically assume that the technology for domesticating plants, having originated in the Middle East, would naturally radiate outward from that location into the rest of the world. This is not what we found. While wheat was being domesticated in the Middle East, rice was being domesticated in Asia. That is not all. Foodstuffs, including beans, squash and maize were being cultivated in Central and South America as early as 8000 BCE.

We find a parallel history in the animal realm. Of the vast variety of vertebrate animals on the planet, only about 40 species of mammals and birds have ever been domesticated. Livestock such as sheep, goats, pigs, cattle and chickens were the first, domesticated as early as 8500 BCE. Animals, domesticated for service, also had a boon in their development. Llamas and alpacas were first domesticated in the Andes Mountains around 4500 BCE. The donkey, domesticated in Northeast Africa, was next. The domestic horse and the Bactrian and dromedary camels followed. This tidbit of information would not be very interesting except for the fact that ALL of the animals that have been bread for the service of mankind appeared between 4500 BCE and 3000 BCE. This trend in plant and animal domestication, despite its geographic disbursement, continued to progress at a rapid pace until about 2500 - 3000 BCE where it all but stopped.

It is believed by scholars that agriculture, as a means of subsistence, is required in order for a civilization to rise. Experts, over the years, have suggested that living a hunter and gatherer lifestyle was difficult and time consuming. It has also been implied that agriculture allowed people to slow down and have more leisure time. Robert Guisepi (Guisepi, 2007) states: "*There was nothing natural or inevitable about the development of agriculture. Because cultivation of plants requires more labor than hunting and gathering...*" But as time went by, for whatever reason, our focus shifted from hunting and gathering to a greater dependence on cultivated crops.

Small groups of hunter-gatherers, who were becoming more reliant on wild grains, began establishing small permanent base camps in which to live. These early village dwellers are referred to as the Natufian Culture, which started to appear around 9000 BCE. Natufian settlements are typically identified by their round semi-subterranean pit-houses. These windowless homes were made of stone with mud plaster floors and a domed roof. Some of the earliest known villages from this culture can be found near the Jordan River in the biblical city of Jericho and at Abu Hureyra in Syria. New technologies, including flint sickles, were being employed to harvest grain. Large storage pits allowed for the collection and long term successful storage of harvested grains. These sites could have supported a population of about 2,000 people.

Building technology and culture quickly spread and advanced. Within 1,500 years a city called Catal Huyuk thrived. Catal Huyuk is located in Turkey and the earliest portions of it date back to about 7500 BCE. It is believed that this early city could have supported a population of 6 - 10,000 people. The people of Catal Huyuk were involved in extensive trade practices. They grew wheat, barley and peas. They smelted and cast lead and tin. Their homes, instead of being made of stone and wood, straw or reeds were made of mud brick that was plastered over. They were also decorated with large brilliantly colored murals and plaster reliefs. Unlike the settlements at Jericho and Abu Hureyra, where the houses were scattered about, the residents of Catal Huyuk lived in what can be likened to a large apartment complex. Houses now featured windows but the homes were packed together closely.

The forerunner of writing is also thought to be associated with the domestication of plants and animals in these early societies. Small tokens of differently shaped pieces of fired clay were used to keep track of livestock, grain and other commodities. Shapes such as cones, disks, cylinders, triangles and tiny balls, some plain, some incised, were used to denote different kinds of wares. For example, a disk with a cross in it might identify a sheep, three cones represented three small units of grain. These tokens allowed individuals to keep better track of their inventory and eventually took the place of the tally stick.

Even though life moved on and cities and cultures developed, mankind took yet another great stride about 3500 BCE with the appearance of "civilization" in Sumer. There are a number of features that separate earlier agriculturally dependent villages and small cities from being identified as a civilized society. Writing, for example, is considered the hallmark of civilization. Writing allows for accurate records to be kept and indicates a complex administrative bureaucracy. Symbols, that represent the fired clay tokens of the past, were incised into clay tablets. The tablets were then baked. This early form of written record keeping is identified as being in the cuneiform style. The use of cuneiform allowed for a more detailed and permanent accounting system. It was not until about 2700 BCE that the use of writing extended past keeping accounting records. This was when a form of cuneiform script broke away and began emulating the spoken word. This gave our early ancestors the first tools to tell their stories, document their past and praise their gods.

Many other characteristics of civilization seemed to have appeared virtually overnight in Sumer. These included astrology, astronomy, the use of the calendar, metallurgy and the wheel. Sumerian cities featured monumental architecture, which is also a fundamental quality associated with a civilization. These cities had a more intricate social structure including ruling classes, priests, artisans and farmers. They possessed a complex market system. Early forms of money, instead of the barter system, became the new medium of exchange for goods, foods and services. The acquisition and ownership of land also moved to the forefront. Successful civilizations, such as in Sumer, began taking over and assimilating the lands of their "less civilized" neighbors through colonization, invasion or religious conversion.

What may have spurred on the dramatic changes in the lifestyle and customs of our ancestors throughout the millennia? Does our mythology provide us with any insights? The Babylonian historian Berosus recounts that the first king to rule the Earth was Alorus. Alorus, according to the text, ruled 432,000 years before the flood, which according to Berosus's accounting of time was 470,530 years ago. This date surprisingly coincides with the emergence of Homo erectus and Neanderthal man. Berosus goes on to state that during the reign of Ammenon, around 377,000 years ago, a creature named Idotion emerged from the Red Sea. Idotion was an "Oannes" or creature from Oannes and is described as being half-man, half-fish. The Oannes are credited with teaching humanity the arts and providing them with moral codes.

The Oannes appeared during the reign of two other kings prior to the flood, during the reign of Daonus some 270,000 years ago and again to Edovanchus 233,000 years ago. Four additional Oannes are reported to have served as advisors to mankind after the deluge.

At first they led a somewhat wretched existence and lived without rule after the manner of beasts. But, in the first year appeared an animal endowed with human reason, named Oannes, who rose from out of the Erythian Sea, at the point where it borders Babylonia. He had the whole body of a fish, but above his fish's head he had another head which was that of a man, and human feet emerged from beneath his fish's tail. He had a human voice, and an image of him is preserved unto this day. He passed the day in the midst of men without taking food; he taught them the use of letters, sciences and arts of all kinds. He taught them to construct cities, to found temples, to compile laws, and explained to them the principles of geometrical knowledge. He made them distinguish the seeds of the earth, and showed them how to collect the fruits; in short he instructed them in everything which could tend to soften human manners and humanize their laws. From that time nothing material has been added by way of improvement to his instructions. And when the sun set, this being Oannes, retired again into the sea, for he was amphibious. After this there appeared other animals like Oannes. - Berossus, from Ancient Fragments - Isaac Preston Cory

In the apocryphal *Book of Enoch*, instead of the gods coming down to Earth to teach man, Enoch ascends into the heavens to study with the "holy sons of God". Enoch is identified in the Bible as being the great-grandfather of Noah. The *Book of Enoch* provides the reader a first- hand account of Enoch's experiences. During his time amongst the sons of God, he is shown the laws of the heavens, the movement of the sun, the moon and the stars in the sky, and the timing of the seasons. Enoch was instructed to teach his children all that he learned within one year, because "*in the second year they shall take thee from their midst*". - Book of Enoch

The Egyptian historian Manetho describes how mankind learned of the movement of the sun, moon and stars.

The Egregori, (Watchers) who had descended to earth in the general cosmic year 1000, held converse with men, and taught them that the orbits of the two luminaries, being marked by the 12 signs of the Zodiac, are composed of 360 parts. - Manetho

Diodorus Siculus, writing in the 1st century BCE reported that the Egyptian goddess Isis discovered wheat, barley and other plants, which were unknown to man growing wildly on the land. Osiris made mankind give up cannibalism and taught them how to cultivate and harvest the fruits of the Earth. Custom still dictated, even at the time of Diodorus's writing, that the first heads of the cut grain were dedicated to the gods.

We find myths containing remarkably analogous elements half a world away. The chronicler Juan de Betanzos (Betanzos, 1996) reported local legends of the earliest times. He informed us that in the very early times the god Viracocha performed many good works. He brought order to the people. He provided them with wise counsel and taught them many things. He left for a length of time and then re-appeared. The Inca were not sure if it was the same god or another who resembled the first. This individual also provided the people with wise counsel and cured the sick.

Garcilaso de la Vega in his *Royal Commentaries of the Incas and General History of Peru* states:

The people lived like wild beasts, with neither order nor religion, neither villages nor houses, neither fields nor clothing, for they had no knowledge of either wool or cotton.

Brought together haphazardly in groups of 2 or 3, they lived in grottoes and caves and like wild game, fed upon grasses and roots, wild fruits, and even human flesh...

Seeing the condition they were in, our father the Sun was ashamed for them, and he decided to send one of his sons and one of his daughters from heaven to earth, in order that they might teach men to adore him and acknowledge him as their god; to obey his laws and precepts as every reasonable creature must do; to build houses and assemble together in villages, to till the soil, sow the seed, raise animals, and enjoy the fruits of the labors like human beings. - Royal Commentaries of the Incas and General History of Peru - Garcilaso de la Vega

The Greeks believed that the gods and heroes taught the primitive humans the art of civilization. The Greek goddess Demeter, for example, taught Triptolemus how to yoke the ox and till the soil. He went on to teach the rest of mankind. In the same manner, we find that the Chinese god Shen Nung taught people to use the plow, sow seeds and utilize plants for their medicinal purposes. The Aztec god Quetzalcoatl instructed his people in the use of metals, agriculture and provided them with a system of laws.

Something we find inexplicable when discussing the evolution of man and his culture are groups such as the aborigines of Australia. Prior to the 1960's, the aborigines showed little sign of advancement. Technologically speaking, they still employ the more primitive Oldowan method for making tools. These semi-nomadic hunter/gatherers never built permanent structures. They had no cities nor large stone monuments. They did not farm nor raise domestic animals. They did not show the outward signs of civilization, yet on the other hand, they maintained all of the elements of a civilized world. They possessed the arts. They had religion. They had a system of law and order. They had music, sang songs and performed dances which told stories of their past. Their culture, on the surface, appears primitive, but it is a mixed bag of science and tradition. With that said, even in Australia we find similar tales regarding the gods and agriculture. Their myths recount stories of the gods teaching them how to gather food using a digging stick and how to harness the power of the spear-thrower.

It was not long before civilization began to appear in other parts of the world. It was a time of profound change. Newgrange, the passage tomb/astrological monument/ritual center in Ireland found its origin in 3200 BCE. Legend holds that Newgrange or *Brú na Bóinne,* the Palace of the Boyne, was the home of Aengus Óg and the Daghdha, the gods of the Tuatha Dé Danaan. In England, the original Stonehenge, Stonehenge I, was constructed around this time. Stonehenge I was a circular earth bank and ditch structure. It is relatively simple when compared to the Stonehenge we see today. The henge at Stonehenge is not the only henge structure to be found in United Kingdom. The United Kingdom is home to 100 henges, all of which date to around 3100 BCE.

In Egypt, 3100 BCE marks the rise of dynastic Egypt. The hallmarks of Egyptian culture took shape during this time including their characteristic art, architecture and religion. According to the current historical timeline, the pyramids were constructed a mere 500 years after the reign of the first pharaoh Menes.

Another amazing coincidence in our mythological history also appears during this period of time. In 3100 BCE or more accurately stated, on February 18, 3102 BCE, according to Hindu tradition, Krishna, the eighth avatar of the god Vishnu vanished from the Earth. Krishna was one of the principal characters in the Indian epic the *Mahabharata*. This date marks the end of the Dvapara Yuga and the beginning of the fourth and final yuga, the Kali Yuga.

India is not the only location that places an emphasis on this period. Stele discovered in Mesoamerica also record the beginning of a new age or cycle. This date is associated with creation in the

Mayan world and the *Planting of the Three-Stone Hearth* myth. Based upon Mayan texts (and a best guess estimate) the beginning of the fifth world commenced on August 11, 3114 BCE.

Oddly enough, a similar date comes to us from Judaism. Jewish tradition states their calendar started in the year of creation. Judaism retains their traditional calendar. As of the time of this writing, we are in the Jewish year 5772, putting creation in the year 3760 BCE. The Jewish calendar has changed in form over the years, but its start in 3760 BCE has been consistently held over the millennia.

Our current method of dating, on the other hand, has changed at least three times through the years. Starting with our original calendar system, it was modified by Julius Caesar (the Julian calendar) and then again by Pope Gregory XIII (the Gregorian calendar). In the process of changing from one calendar system to the next, days, months and perhaps years were lost. Thus, when we try to date an event using a native calendar system and then look to convert it to our own Gregorian calendar, problems can occur. This could account for the discrepancies seen above in the dates provided.

Regardless of their precision, the close proximity of the dates (+/- less than 1,000 years) and the associated mythos is still rather remarkable. The question we ask is what happened between 3800 and 3100 BCE that was so important that multiple cultures commemorate this date and associate it with a new start. Some experts surmise that our ancestors memorialized the advent of civilization. It is hard for us to imagine that a civilization would decide in foresight that they have achieved all of the makings of civilization and then write it onto their calendars. One thing is certain. This period marks the end of the Fourth World and the beginning of the Fifth Age, our current world.

Our journey back through time on the wings of some of the world's oldest and greatest myths ends with the beginning of the Fifth World and the advent of civilization. The introduction of the written word provided us with the opportunity to document our lives and our history. Writing also allowed us to record the accounts of the gods who once walked the Earth.

Are the gods the forces of nature or figments or our ancestor's imagination? Synchronicities, parallels in time and the consistency in the myths from around the world have led us to one conclusion: The gods who came to this Earth and created life on this planet were living breathing beings. When we ask how we can know and understand the gods of lore, we need only to look at ourselves. The traditions we keep, the morals we live by, and the world we see around us are a direct reflection of these extraterrestrial beings.

Epilog - Unnatural Selection

Today, we find ourselves looking up at the stars and asking questions like: Who are we? Where do we come from? Why are we here? These questions have been pondered from time immemorial. We see ourselves as alone in the universe, as the caretakers of the Earth and the masters of our destiny. Mythology tells a very different story regarding our place in the world. We, contrary to popular belief, are but a footnote in the action, adventures and scandals of the gods. In Sumerian literature, for example, members of the human race, the black-headed people, are never described as being equal to the gods.

In other cultures, man in his present form is rarely mentioned in myth. In ancient tales such as the Indian epic the *Ramayana* we find characters like Hanuman, the mighty ape-man who aids Rama in his battles against evil in the world. In the *Epic of Gilgamesh*, we meet the hair-covered primitive man Enkidu, Gilgamesh's constant companion and friend. The gods created Enkidu. He is ignorant of human culture and is described as eating grass with the gazelles and drinking water at watering holes with the cattle and other wild beasts. The story goes on to tell us that after a period spent with humans he takes on a certain level of civilization and culture. The same attributes are associated with the monkey god Sun Hou-tzu. Sun Hou-tzu traveled the Earth for eighteen years and eventually acquired human attributes. Even though his face and general physical appearance never changed, he dressed in human apparel and became civilized.

Are these tales talking about a primitive form of man? Could the ape-men referred to in these stories be depictions of our ancestors when seen through the eyes of the gods? The concept of the evolution of man from a single celled organism to its current form has been fiercely contested ever since Charles Darwin released his classic book *The Origin Of The Species*. It has long been proposed that all life started as a mixture of inorganic substances in chemical rich pond, the primordial soup. Lightning, or some say heat, brought these simple molecules to life forming the first amino acids, the building blocks of life. Statistical analysis of life on Earth beginning this way, according to mathematician and astronomer Sir Frederick Hoyle, are about 10^{40000}. Hoyle states, *"The chance that higher life forms might have emerged in this way is comparable to the chance that a tornado sweeping through a junkyard might assemble a Boeing 747 from the materials therein."*

We do not discount the possibility of miracles, but all life on Earth has experienced a number of miraculous changes that the Theory of Evolution has yet to explain. When the Theory of Evolution is applied to humankind, scientists still scratch their heads when they run into the question of the missing link. Somehow, we have been transformed from ape-like brutes into conscious, sentient beings capable of culture and reasoning. Did man advance and evolve naturally as the Theory of Evolution suggests or was there something else going on?

Genetic research into the development and evolution of man has yielded some amazing discoveries. Our genetic material, according to scholars, is responsible for behavioral changes such as the development of language and culture. For example, the FOXP2 gene is associated with our ability to speak and use language. It is not exclusive to human beings. It can be found in most multi-cellular organisms including extremely simple life forms like fungi. This gene has developed over the millennia and has undergone three major changes to its form in the last 70 million years. Two of the changes occurred solely in the human lineage. These unique mutations have been identified to have taken place around 200,000 years ago. This date converges with the rise of anatomically modern humans. What is interesting is that these same mutations have been found in Neanderthal DNA, while they are not present in our nearest living relative, the chimpanzee.

The MHPH gene is another gene associated with modern man. It is responsible for the regulation of brain size. The brain size of early hominids (7 to 2 million years ago) did not vary. By 2 million years ago hominid brain sizes had doubled from the size of the great apes to the size of the typical modern human brain. It is believed that mutations to the MHPH gene were the cause of this change. The MHPH gene is represented by six versions, but as research continues, that number is growing. Based upon the genetic diversity of this gene, it is believed that versions one through five originated around 1.7 million years ago. This parallels the rise of Homo erectus, our tool using and fire-controlling ancestor. We can only assume that the Neanderthals also possessed this same genetic structure.

Interestingly, about 37,000 years ago mankind began to express a variation of the MHPH gene called haplogroup D. It has spread to become the most common form throughout the world except in Sub-Saharan Africa. What makes the emergence of haplogroup D so fascinating is its appearance astonishingly correlates to the emergence of behaviorally modern man and the creative explosion.

The coincidences do not end there. Human DNA's most recent advancement was with a mutation associated with the ASPM gene. The ASPM gene is associated with regulating the size of the cerebral cortex of the brain. This new version of the gene is estimated to have appeared somewhere between 5,000 and 10,000 years ago. While scientists are still not quite sure how this gene affects us, its appearance during this time puts it at the advent of our version of civilization. Call it what you will, but the dating of the genetic changes we have experienced seem too coincidental and too miraculous to have been natural.

Could the changes that are seen in the evolution of mankind been spurred so we might better serve the gods as the Sumerian texts seem to suggest? Carleton Stevens Coon (Coon, 1939) states that man is the oldest domesticated animal on the planet. Could that possibly be true? Could we have been bred to be of service to the gods?

The concept of domestication implies that a population of plants or animals is manipulated through a process of artificial selection, changing the species at the genetic level, and over time displaying the desired traits. When we think of domesticated animals, our minds often envision cattle as they graze in open pastures. Domestic animals are often used as a source of meat, dairy or fiber (hair/wool, skin/leather). Another group of animals that have been domesticated are ones used for labor such as horses and donkeys.

Evolutionary biologist, Jared Diamond, has identified six criteria that must been met in order to domesticate a species successfully. They include a flexible diet, a reasonably fast growth rate, the ability to be bred in captivity, a pleasant disposition and a calm temperament. They also require a modifiable social hierarchy. This means that domesticated animals, such as dogs, can be raised to recognize humans as their dominant pack leaders. Animals, once domesticated, as a sort of side effect, display an increased need to be cared for in order to stay alive and productive.

Juliet Clutton-Brock (Clutton-Brock, 1999) identifies another aspect of domestication - culture. Cultural domestication is defined as a way of life imposed over a society by successive generations. According to Clutton-Brock, domestication causes imbalances and disruptions in the rate of growth of an organism. She has found that in the early stages of domestication the overall body size of the animal is reduced. Changes to the facial region of the skull and jaw are also seen, with their facial features becoming smaller or flatter as seen in a juvenile of the same species. The teeth in domesticated animals also shrink in size. Deposits of body fat in domestic animals build up under the skin and through the muscles verses being stored around the organs as is seen in wild animals of the same species. Hair color and type exhibit a more striking range of differences and in many animals;

they develop floppy ears and curly tails. Finally, the brain size, relative to body size, decreases in domestic mammals.

Did our brains begin to shrink once the process of domestication began? Did the gods, when they noticed the problem, intervene and introduced the MHPH gene to increase our cranium (brain) size? Was our DNA manipulated in order to support the plans of the gods? Did they give us knowledge of fire and tools because we were becoming increasingly dependent and were less able to survive in the wild on our own?

John Hawks, of the University of Wisconsin, has found that over the past 20,000 years, the size of our brains have begun to decrease. Some researchers believe that our brains have shrunk in size because we have become more efficient thinkers. Others believe that it is blatant proof that we have tamed ourselves. David Geary and Drew Bailey of the University of Missouri found that population density also closely correlates with brain size. When populations were low, our cranium kept getting bigger. Starting about 15,000 years ago, as more complex societies began to emerge, our brains began to get smaller. Is it because we did not have to be as smart to stay alive? Other investigations into cranium size have revealed that since the dawn of the Bronze Age, some 4,000 years ago, our brains have been shrinking even faster.

What may have caused our brain volume to be reduced, proposes Richard Wrangham, a primatologist at Harvard University is that we have selected out the characteristic of aggression from the population. Wrangham refers to a 1958 experiment performed by Russian geneticist Dmitri Belyaev. Belyaev raised silver foxes in captivity. When two animals were bred, he selected only the animals that showed the most positive responses to humans. The animals began to show evidence of physical traits associated with domestication after a mere 12 generations. These animals, a few generations later, acted more like domesticated dogs than their wild counterparts. They also developed smaller skeletons, had white spots on their fur, floppy ears and curly tails.

In mankind, the selection for a less aggressive breed occurred through the enactment of laws, rules, regulations and customs that prevail within each culture. They form the foundation for what we call society. Wrangham theorizes that when someone exhibited aggressive tendencies in these early cultures, the person was killed or expelled from the community. This, like the silver foxes, would change the genetic profile within the group and go on to advance our total domestication.

Who made up the rules of human behavior? Mythology tells us the gods gave us the laws by which we live. God, after the flood, is reported to have provided Noah with seven laws or seven commandments to obey. They are known as the Noahide Laws and are seen as universal laws. In 1991, a joint resolution of the United States Congress called its principles *"the bedrock of society from the dawn of civilization..."* The oldest written set of laws known to date is the *Code of Urukagina*. It was complied around 2600 BCE. Urukagina was the leader of Lagash. His laws sought to reform the oppressions of the current government and preserve the rights of property owners. The laws and reforms proposed by Urukagina were designed to return the society (according to Samuel Noah Kramer) to the *"original social order decreed by the gods."* Religion, superstition, greed, power and control have held these laws in place over the years ensuring the inevitability of our domestication.

It is a precept of science to discover new things. If, however, these discoveries do not fit into the status quo, then the data is often adjusted to fit our current beliefs or dismissed. It was not so long ago that we believed that the Earth was the center of the universe. Some scientists still suggest that we are the pinnacle of life in the cosmos. Recent discoveries into the nature of the universe have caused our understanding of our place in it to shift. The belief that man (as the only form of intelligent life in the universe and the sole intelligent creation of a singular god) is being challenged. Many have come to recognize that we are actually part of something bigger, grander and perhaps on a scale we are yet able to comprehend.

In the inception of this book, we decided to make every effort to avoid such things as UFO's, aliens, time warps and other concepts that may not have a rational scientific explanation. In analyzing the myths, tales and stories of man carefully and then comparing them to scientific and historical documents, we became stuck in the quagmire of reality. The more we dug, the more we found ourselves being forced down a funnel to envision a new reality. By applying the principal of Ockham's razor, that proposes that when you have two competing theories the simpler one is better, we came to a conclusion that we believe goes beyond speculation. Humanity, when looked at through the lens of mythology seems less a product of chance and circumstances and more like you, me, all of us have been Man-Made...

man-made /măn'mād'/ - *adjective:* manufactured; synthetic; made artificially; not occurring in nature

Bibliography

"A Hot Big Bang." *The University Of Wisconsin, Madison, Observational Cosmology.*
http://cmb.physics.wisc.edu/tutorial/bigbang.html (accessed 2011).
   Guisepi, Robert, ed. "Agriculture And The Origins Of Civilization: The Neolithic Revolution." *International World History Project.* 2007. http://history-world.org/agriculture.htm (accessed 2012).
   Alexander, Amir. "Ancient Asteroid Storm May Have Aided The Emergence Of Life." *Roy Wright's Informal Learning Blog.* May 29, 2009. http://rwainternational.us/?p=137 (accessed 2011).
   Anitei, Stefan. "The Suicide Neanderthal Blonde." *Softpedia.* October 26, 2007. http://news.softpedia.com/news/The-Suicide-Neanderthal-Blond-69221.shtml (accessed August 20, 2010).
   Atsma, Aaron J. *Theoi Greek Mythology.* 2011. http://www.theoi.com/ (accessed 2011).
   Bancroft, Hubert Howe. *The Native Races Of The Pacific States.* New York: Appleton and Company, 1875.
   Bellows, Henry Adams, trans. *The Poetic Edda.* Princeton: Princeton University Press, 1936.
   Bennett, Chris. "Soma revealed." *Cannabis Culture*, January 12, 2004.
   Berens, E.M. *Myths And Legends Of Ancient Greece And Rome.* New York: Maynard, Merrill, & Co., 1894.
   Betanzos, Juan De. *Narrative Of The Incas.* Edited by Dana Buchanan. Translated by Roland Hamilton. Austin, TX: University of Texas Press, 1996.
   Bibring, Jean-Pierre. "Mars Express Evidence For Large Aquifers On Early Mars." *European Space Agency.* November 30, 2005.

http://www.esa.int/SPECIALS/Results_from_Mars_Express_and_Huygens
/SEMA1UULWFE_0.html (accessed 2011).
    Black, J.A., Cunningham, G., Ebeling, J., Flückiger-Hawker, E.,
Robson, E., Taylor, J., and Zólyomi, G.,. "Enki And Ninmah." *Electronic
Text Corpus of Sumerian Literature.* 1998.
http://etcsl.orinst.ox.ac.uk/section1/tr112.htm (accessed 2010).
    —. "Enki And The World Order." *The Electronic Text Corpus of
Sumerian Literature.* 1998.
http://etcsl.orinst.ox.ac.uk/section1/tr113.htm (accessed 2010).
    —. "Gilgamesh And Aga." *The Electronic Text Corpus of Sumerian
Literature.* 1998. http://etcsl.orinst.ox.ac.uk/section1/tr1811.htm
(accessed 2010).
    —. "How Grain Came To Sumer." *The Electronic Text Corpus of
Sumerian Literature.* 1998. http://etcsl.orinst.ox.ac.uk/cgi-
bin/etcsl.cgi?text=t.1.7.6&charenc=j# (accessed 2010).
    —. "Inana And Enki." *The Electronic Text Corpus of Sumerian
Literature.* 1998. http://etcsl.orinst.ox.ac.uk/section1/tr131.htm
(accessed 2010).
    —. "Inana And Shu-kale-tuda." *The Electronic Text Corpus of
Sumerian Literature .* 1998.
http://etcsl.orinst.ox.ac.uk/section1/tr133.htm (accessed 2010).
    —. "Nanna-Suen's Journey To Nibru." *Electronic Text Corpus of
Sumerian Literature.* 1998. http://etcsl.orinst.ox.ac.uk/cgi-
bin/etcsl.cgi?text=t.1.5.1&charenc=j# (accessed 2010).
    —. "Ninurta's Exploits." *The Electronic Text Corpus of Sumerian
Literature.* 1998. http://etcsl.orinst.ox.ac.uk/cgi-
bin/etcsl.cgi?text=t.1.6.2# (accessed 2010).
    —. "Ninurta's Return To Nibru." *The Electronic Text Corpus of
Sumerian Literature.* December 19 2006. http://etcsl.orinst.ox.ac.uk/cgi-
bin/etcsl.cgi?text=t.1.6.1# (accessed 2010).
    —. "Rulers Of Lagash." *Electronic Text Corpus of Sumerian
Literature.* 1998. http://etcsl.orinst.ox.ac.uk/section2/tr212.htm
(accessed 2010).
    —. "The Exploits Of Ninurta." *The Electronic Text Corpus of
Sumerian Literature.* 1998.
http://etcsl.orinst.ox.ac.uk/section1/tr162.htm.
    —. "The Flood Story." *The Electronic Text Corpus of Sumerian
Literature .* 1998. http://etcsl.orinst.ox.ac.uk/cgi-
bin/etcsl.cgi?text=t.1.7.4&charenc=j# (accessed 2010).

—. "The Song Of The Hoe: Translation." *The Electronic Text Corpus of Sumerian Literature.* 1998. http://etcsl.orinst.ox.ac.uk/section5/tr554.htm (accessed January 8, 2011).

—. "The Sumerian King List." *The Electronic Text Corpus of Sumerian Literature.* 1998. http://etcsl.orinst.ox.ac.uk/section2/tr211.htm (accessed 2010).

Fisher, Suzanne D., ed. "Books Of The Chilam Balam Of Chumayel." *Ancient Wisdom.* 2005. http://myweb.cableone.net/subru/Chilam.html#anchor933551 (accessed August 3, 2010).

Brinton, Daniel G. *American Hero-Myths.* Philadelphia: H. C. Watts & Co., 1882.

—. *Annals of the Cakchiquels.* Philadelphia: Brinton's Library Of Aboriginal American Literature, 1885.

—. *The Myths Of The New World.* Philadelphia: David McKay, 1905.

Brodeur, Arthur Gilchrist, trans. *The Prose Edda Of Snorri Sturlson.* New York: The American-Scandinavian Foundation, 1916.

Brown, Abbie Farwell. *In The Days Of Giants; A Book Of Norse Tales.* Boston: Houghton Mifflin Co, 1902.

Budge, E. A. Wallis. *Legends Of The Gods.* London: Trench and Trübner & Co. Ltd., 1912.

—. *The Babylonian Legends Of Creation.* London: Harrison and Sons, ltd., 1921.

Buess, Lynn. *Numerology for the New Age.* Flagstaff: Light Technology Publications, 1978.

Bulfinch, Thomas. *Bulfinch's Mythology.* 1855.

Caesarea, Eusebius of. *Eusebius' Chronicle.* Translated by Robert Bedrosian.

Callaway, Henry. *The Religious System of the Amazulu.* The Folk-Lore Society, 1870.

Cambridge, trans. *Legends Of The Gods.* London: Trench and Trübner & Co. Ltd., 1912.

Jason And The Argonauts. Directed by Don Chaffey. 1963.

Chamberlain, Basil Hall, trans. *The Kojiki.* 1919.

Chamberlain, Basil Hall, trans. *The Kojiki.* 1919.

Charles, R. H., trans. *The Book of Jubilees.* London: Society for Promoting Christian Knowledge, 1917.

Charles, R.H., trans. *The Book Of Enoch.* London: Society for Promoting Christian Knowledge, 1917.

Choi, Charles Q. *Astrobiology Magazine* . December 09, 2010. http://www.astrobio.net/exclusive/3706/the-three-ages-of-mars (accessed 2012).

Clutton-Brock, Juliet. *A Natural History Of Domesticated Mammals.* Cambridge: Cambridge University Press, 1999.

Column, Padraic. *Orpheus: Myths of the World.* New York: The Macmillan Company, 1930.

Coon, Carleton Sevens. *The Races Of Europe.* New York: The MacMillan Company, 1939.

Coon, Carleton Stevens. *The Races Of Europe.* New York: The MacMillan Company, 1939.

Cory, Isaac Preston. *Ancient Fragments.* London: Pickering, 1828.

Crystal, Ellie. *Crystalinks.* http://www.crystalinks.com (accessed 2010).

Davis, Frederick Hadland. *Myths & legends Of Japan.* New York: Thomas Y. Crowell Company, 1912.

DuBose, Hampden C. *Dragon, Image, And Demon.* London: S. W. Partridge and Co. , 1886.

Durham University . "Early Star Formation In The Universe Illuminated." *ScienceDaily.* September 13, 2007. http://www.sciencedaily.com /releases/2007/09/070913140318.htm (accessed 2010).

Bratcher, Dennis, ed. *Enuma Elish: "When on High . . .".* http://crivoice.org/enumaelish.html (accessed 2011).

Evelyn-White, Hugh G., trans. *Hesiod: Works And Days.* Cambridge: Harvard University Press, 1914.

Evelyn-White, Hugh G., trans. *The Theogony Of Hesiod.* 1914.

Evelyn-White, Hugh G., trans. *The Theogony Of Hesiod.* 1914.

Faraday, L. Winifred. *The Edda.* London: David Nutt, 1902.

Fisher, Suzanne D., trans.

Frankfurt, Harry. "Homo Erectus." *Human Evolution.* http://www.stanford.edu/~harryg/protected/chp22.htm (accessed 2012).

Gamboa, Pedro Sarmiento De. *History Of The Incas.* Translated by Clements Markham. The Hakluyt Society, 1907.

Garcia, Erik Velasquez. "The Maya Flood Myth And The Decapitation of The Cosmic Caiman." *PARI Journal*, 2006: 1-10.

Gill, Sam D. *Storytracking: Texts, Stories, And Histories In Central Australia* . Oxford University Press, 1998.

Gilligan, Gary. "Re (Ra), the Egyptian Red Sun God?" *The God King Scenario.* http://www.gks.uk.com/sun-god-ra/ (accessed 2011).

"Gold During The Classical Period." March 2011. http://www.minelinks.com/alluvial/goldClassic.html (accessed August 8, 2011).

Griaule, Marcel and Dieterlen, Germaine. *The Dogon.* London: Oxford University Press, 1954.

Griffith, Ralph T. H. *Ramayan Of Valmiki.* London: Benares: E. J. Lazarus and Co., 1870.

Guerber, H. A. *Myths of the Norsemen.* London: George G. Harrap & Company, 1909.

Hallo, William W. "Antediluvian Cities." *Journal of Cuneiform Studies* (The American Schools of Oriental Research) 23, no. 3 (1971): 57-67.

Harlan, Jack R. *Crops & Man.* Second Edition. Madison: American Society of Agronomy-Crop Science Society, 1992.

Harrison, R. K. "Reinvestigating The Antediluvian Sumerian King List." *Journal for the Evangelical Study of the Old Testament*, March 1993: 3-8.

Henning, W. B., trans. *The Book Of The Giants.* Forgotten Books, 2007.

"Important Scientists: Georges Lemaitre." *Physics Of The Universe.* 2009. http://www.physicsoftheuniverse.com/scientists_lemaitre.html (accessed 2010).

Indian Divinity. 2012. http://www.webonautics.com/ (accessed November 17, 2011).

Klah, Hasteen. *Navaho Creation Myth.* Santa Fe: Navajo Religion Series, 1942.

Kramer, Samuel Noah. *Sumerian Mythology.* Philadelphia: University of Pennsylvania Press, 1961.

Lang, Andrew. *Myth, Ritual and Religion.* London: Longmans, Green and Co., 1913.

Langdon, Stephen. *Sumerian And Semitic Religious And Historical Texts.* London: Oxford University Press, 1923.

LaRocco, Chris and Rothstein, Blair. "The Big Bang: It Sure Was Big!!" *University Of Michigan.* http://www.umich.edu/~gs265/bigbang.htm (accessed 2011).

Leeming, David Adams. *The World Of Myth.* New York: Oxford University Press, 1990.

Leon, Pedro De Cieza De. *The Travels Of Pedro De Cieza De Leon.* Translated by Clements R. Markham. The Hakluyt Society, 1864.

Lerner, K. Lee and Lerner, Brenda Wilmoth, ed. *World Of Earth Science.* Gale, 2002.

Lindemans, Micha F. "Seraphim." *Encyclopedia Mythica from Encyclopedia Mythica Online.* May 24, 2011. http://www.pantheon.org/articles/s/seraphim.html.

Lockett, Hattie Greene. *The Unwritten Literature Of The Hopi.* Tucson: University of Arizona, 1933.

Mackenzie, Donald A. *Myths of Babylonia And Assyria.* London: Gresham Publishing Company, 1915.

Mackenzie, Donald Alexander. *Indian Myth and Legend.* London: Gresham Publishing Company, 1913.

Markham, Clements R., trans. *Narratives Of The Rites And Laws Of The Yncas.* London, 1873.

Markman, Peter T. Markman and Roberta H. *Masks of the Spirit: Image and Metaphor in Mesoamerica.* Berkeley: University Of California Press, 1989.

Marusek, James A. "Ice Age Impact And The Great Flood." *Cambridge-Conference Network* , 2003.

Mooney, James. *Myths Of The Cherokee.* Nineteenth Annual Report of the Bureau of American Ethnology to the Secretary of the Smithsonian Institution, 1897.

Morgan, Elaine. "Aquatic Ape Theory." *Primitivism.* http://www.primitivism.com/aquatic-ape.htm (accessed 2010).

Morris, Desmond. *The Naked Ape: A Zoologist's Study Of The Human Animal.* New York: McGraw-Hill Book Company, 1967.

Morton, G.R. *Subterranean Mining and Religion in Ancient Man.* 1996. http://home.entouch.net/dmd/mining.htm (accessed 2011).

Museum, British. *The Babylonian Legends Of The Creation.* Order Of The Trustees, 1921.

Niels Bohr Institute. *Evolutionary History Of Mars.* http://www.nbi.ku.dk/forskningsgrupper/mars/english/mars/evolution/ (accessed January 7, 2012).

O'Neil, Dennis. *Evolution Of Modern Humans.* 2011. http://anthro.palomar.edu/homo2/mod_homo_3.htm (accessed 2011).

Opler, Morris Edward. "Myths and Tales of the Jicarilla Apache Indians." *Memoirs of the American Folklore Society* 31 (1938): 406.

Orchard, Andy. *Dictionary Of Norse Myth And Legend*. London: Cassell, 1997.

Paterson, Nicolas, and Ronald J. Lampert. "A Central Australian Ochre Mine ." *The Australian Museum*, 1985: 1-9.

Pinches, Theophilus G. *The Old Testament In The Light Of The Historical Records And Legends Of Assyria And Babylonia* . London: Society For Promoting Christian Knowledge, 1908.

—. *The Religion of Babylonia and Assyria*. Archibald Constable & Co. Ltd., 1906.

Read, Molly. "A Hot Big Bang." *What Is The Ultimate Fate Of The Universe?* http://cmb.physics.wisc.edu/tutorial/bigbang.html (accessed 2010).

Roan, Shari. "Social Stigma Drives Some Women to Remove Tattoos." *Las Angeles Times*. 21 2008, July. http://latimesblogs.latimes.com/booster_shots/2008/07/social-stigma-d.html (accessed 2010).

Rogers, R. W. *Adapa And The Food Of Life* . 1912.

Rogers, R. W., trans. *Adapa And The Food Of Life*. 1912.

Roys, Ralph L., ed. *The Book Of Chilam Balam Of Chumayel*. Washington D.C., 1933.

Saraswati, Swami Satyadharma. "The Ten Avataras: A Psychological Study Of The Evolution Of Humankind." *Yoga Magazine*, 2006.

Shestople, Paul. "Big Bang Cosmology Primer." *Berkeley Cosmology Group*. December 24, 1997. http://cosmology.berkeley.edu/Education/IUP/Big_Bang_Primer.html (accessed 2011).

Simonite, Tom. "Ancient Genetic Tricks Shape Up Wheat." *Nature*. January 3, 2006. http://www.nature.com/news/2006/060102/full/news060102-2.html (accessed May 25, 2011).

Smith, George. *Chaldean Account of Genesis*. London: Thomas Scott, 1876.

—. *History Of Babylonia*. London: Society For Promoting Christian Knowledge.

Smyth, Robert Brough. *The Aborigines Of Victoria*. London: Trubner and Co., 1878.

Spence, Lewis. *The Myths of Mexico and Peru*. London: George Harrp, 1913.

—. *The Myths Of the North American Indians.* New York: Crowell Company, 1914.

Spencer, Baldwin. *The Native Tribes Of Central Australia.* London: MacMillan and Co. Limited, 1899.

"Sri Brahma-samhita." *Bhaktivedanta VedaBase Network.* http://vedabase.net (accessed 2011).

"Srimad Bhagavatam." *Bhaktivedanta VedaBase Network.* http://www.vedabase.net (accessed 2011).

Stead, Lewis. *Ravenbok: The Raven Kindred Ritual Book.* Wheaton: Asatru Today, 1994.

Taylor, Rob. "Ancient Stone Tools Found On Australia Mine Site." *Reuters.* April 7, 2008. http://www.reuters.com/article/2008/04/07/us-australia-aborigines-idUSSYD23232520080407 (accessed August 11, 2011).

"Teachings of Lord Caitanya." *Bhaktivedanta VedaBase Network.* http://vedabase.net/tlc/14/en1 (accessed 2010).

The Book Of Jasher. Salt Lake city: J. H. Parry & Company, 1887.

"The Epic Of Atrahasis." *Livius.Org.* May 11 2007. http://www.livius.org/as-at/atrahasis/atrahasis.html (accessed August 16, 2011).

"The Epic of Gilgamesh." *Academy For Ancient Texts.* http://www.ancienttexts.org/library/mesopotamian/gilgamesh/ (accessed November 29, 2011).

The Eridu Genesis. May 10, 2007. http://www.livius.org/ei-er/eridu/eridu_genesis.html (accessed August 16, 2011).

The Gnostic Society. *Gnostic Society Library.* 2001. http://www.gnosis.org (accessed 2011).

"The Navajo Creation Story ." *USC Research Computing Facility.* http://www-bcf.usc.edu/~lapahie/Creation.html (accessed 2010).

Fisher, Suzanne D., ed. "The Popol Vuh." *Ancient Wisdom.* http://myweb.cableone.net/subru/Mayan.html (accessed August 3, 2010).

Fisher, Suzanne D., ed. "The Popol Vuh." *Ancient Wisdom.* 2005. http://myweb.cableone.net/subru/Mayan.html (accessed August 3, 2010).

Thomas, W. J. *Some Myths And Legends Of The Australian Aborigines.* London: Whitcombe & Tombs Limited, 1923.

"Three Sovereigns And Five Emperors." *New World Encyclopedia.*

Tranberg, Dustin. "Soma And The Mead Of Poetry." *Lady Of The Earth.* December 10 1992.
http://www.ladyoftheearth.com/lessons/soma.txt (accessed 2011).

Vega, Garcilaso de la. *Royal Commentaries of the Incas.* University of Texas Press, 1966.

—. *Royan Commentaries Of The Incas.* Translated by Harold V. Livermore. Indianapolis: Hackett Publishing Company, Inc., 2006.

Vyasa, Krishna Dwaipayana. *The Mahabharata.* Translated by Kisari Mohan Ganguli.

Wallis, Henry White. *The Cosmology Of The Rigveda.* London: Williams and Norgate, 1887.

Wasson, Robert Gordon. *Soma: Divine Mushroom of Immortality.* New York: Houghton Mifflin Harcourt, 1972.

Waters, Frank. *Book Of The Hopi.* Penguin Books, 1977.

Werner, Alice. *Myths And Legends Of The Bantu.* London: George W. Harrap and Co., 1933.

Werner, Edward T.C. *Myths And Legends Of China.* London: George G. Harrap & Co. Ltd. , 1922.

Wilson, Horace Hayman, trans. *The Vishnu Purana.* London: John Murray, 1840.

Wirth, Diane. "The Seven Primordial Tribes." *The New Archaeology Review*, 2006: 10 - 15.

Other Titles By
Rita Louise, PhD

Dark Angels: An Insider's Guids To Ghosts, Spirits &
Attached Entities

Avoiding The Cosmic 2x4

The Power Within

All of these titles are available through www.SoulHealer.com

CPSIA information can be obtained at www.ICGtesting.com
Printed in the USA
LVOW132327041012

301596LV00001B/1/P